LARGE PRINT
Peaceful
Dot-to-Dot

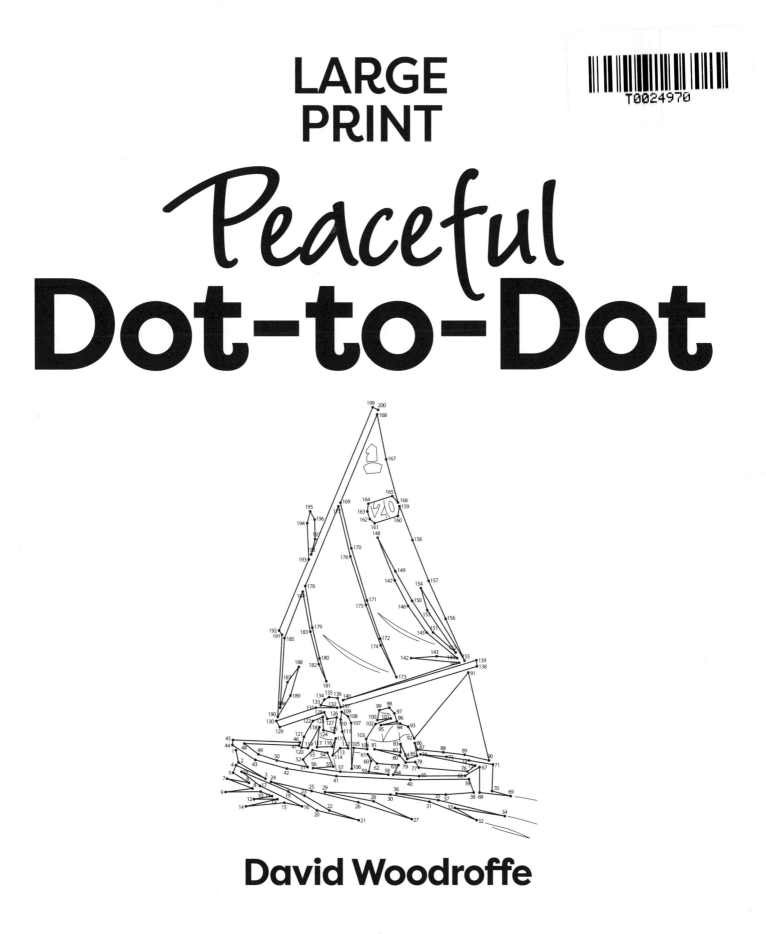

David Woodroffe

SIRIUS

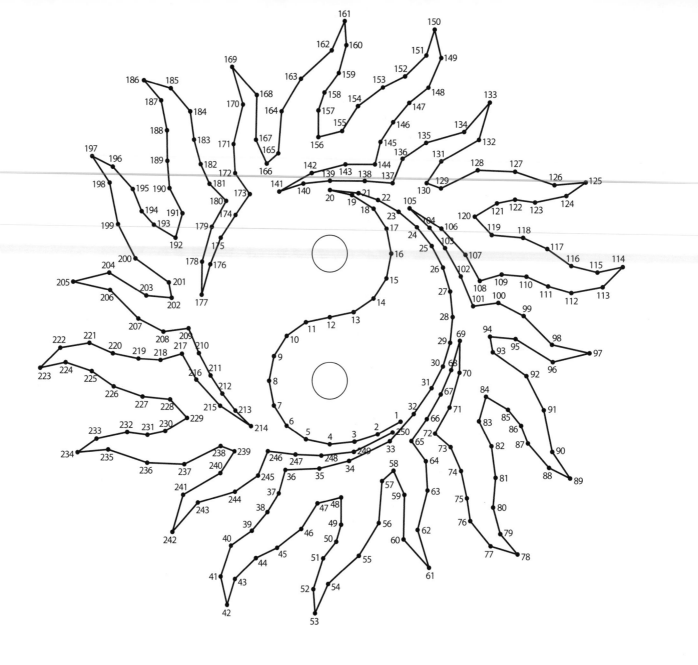

SIRIUS

This edition published in 2022 by Sirius Publishing, a division of
Arcturus Publishing Limited,
26/27 Bickels Yard, 151–153 Bermondsey Street,
London SE1 3HA

ISBN: 978-1-3988-2037-1
CH010354NT
Supplier 29, Date 0522, PI 00001705

Printed in China

LARGE PRINT

Peaceful
Dot-to-Dot

Introduction

What could be simpler than following the numbers and joining the dots in these delightful puzzles. Yes, you do need to concentrate – the numbers aren't always right next to one another – but you will find that as you focus on revealing the image, you forget many of your day-to-day cares.

All the subjects depicted have been specially chosen: from famous people to animals, mindful symbols, works of art and our natural world. As you complete the image, it is worth reflecting on what it has taken to create the figure in front of you – whether it be the cycle of life or the product of our imagination. Every object is a powerful reminder of the wonderful world in which we live.

So, grab your pencil – and perhaps some crayons if you want to add some extra touches to the images when you have joined all the dots – and settle down to enjoy revealing the pictures in the following pages.

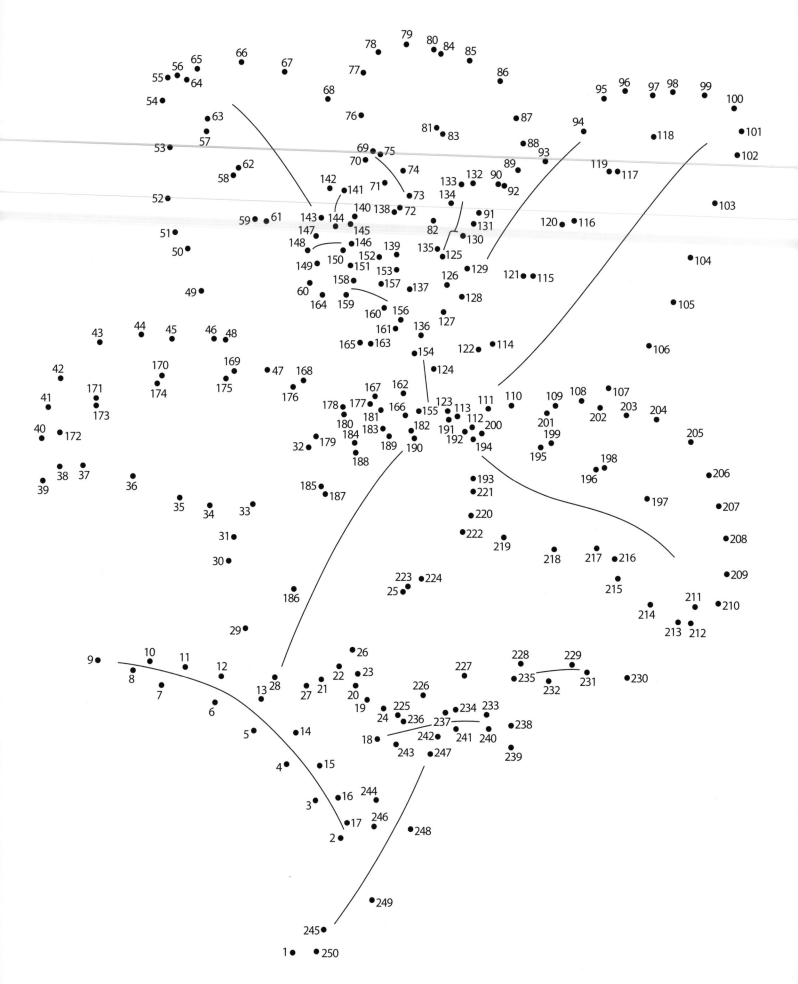

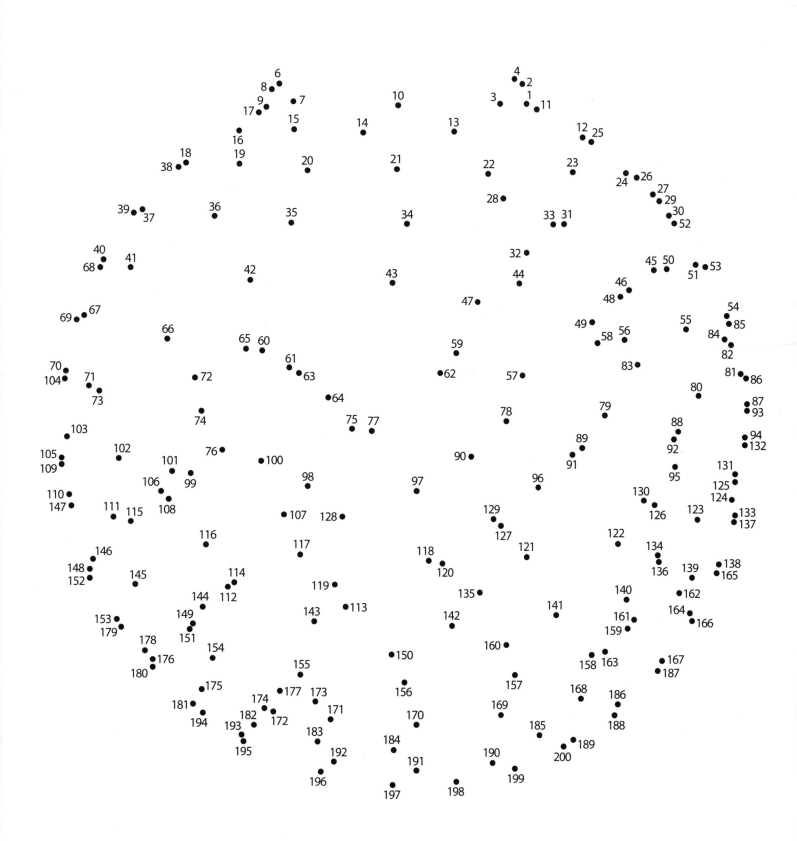

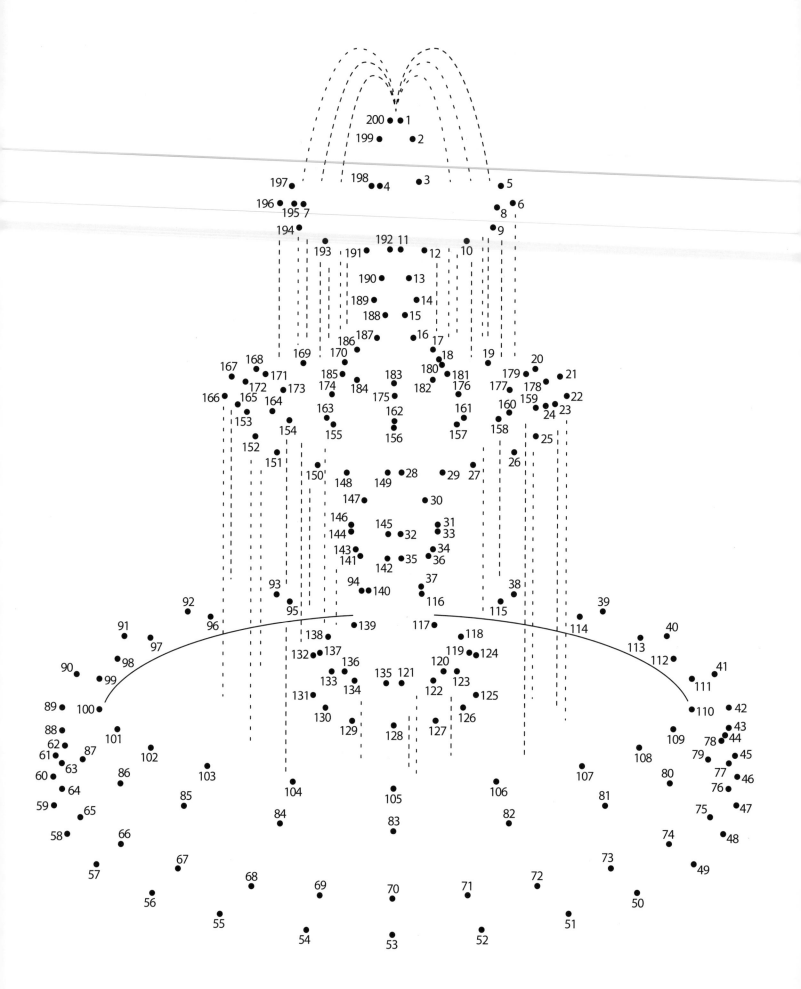

8

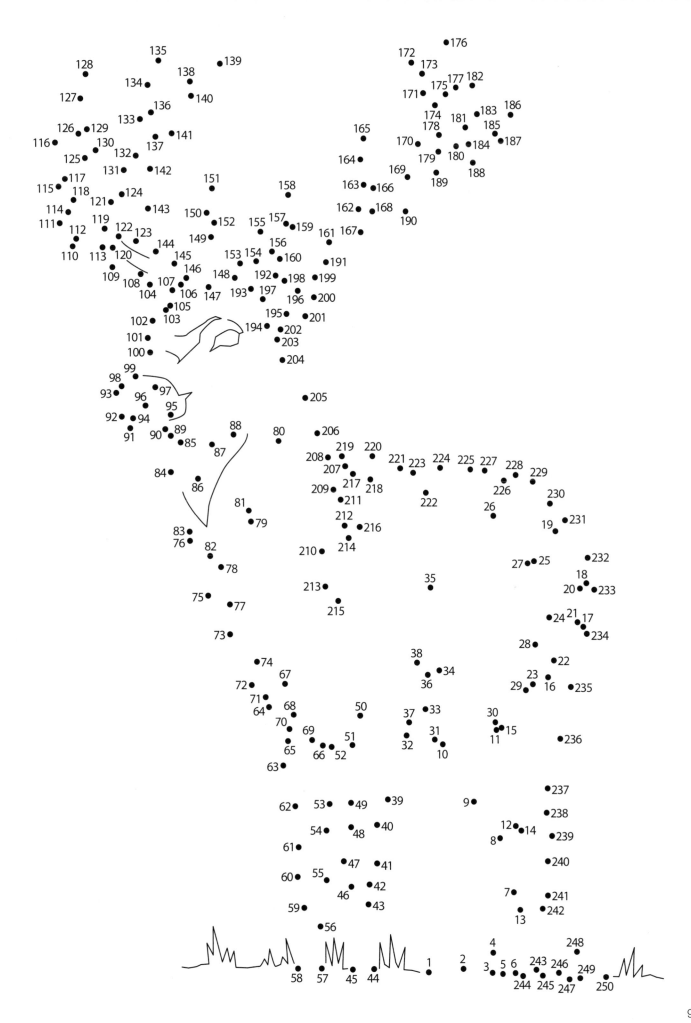

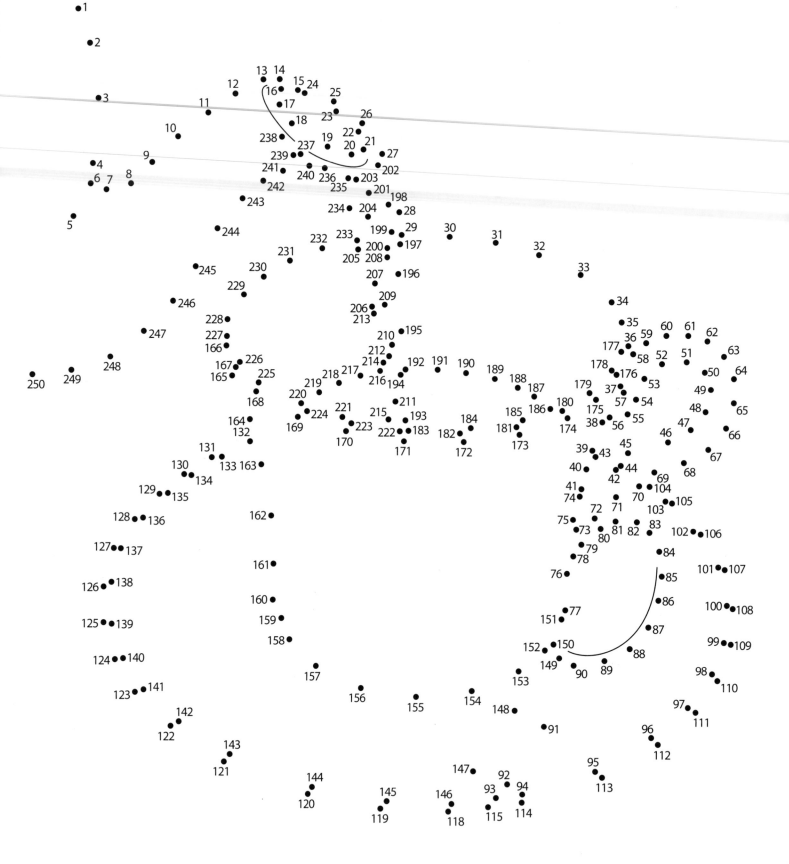

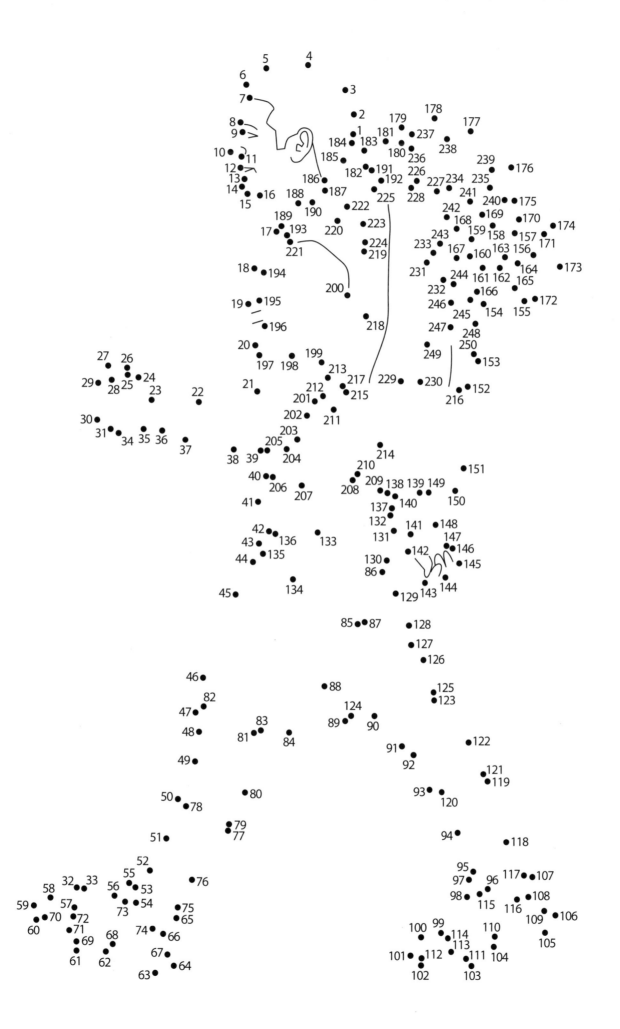

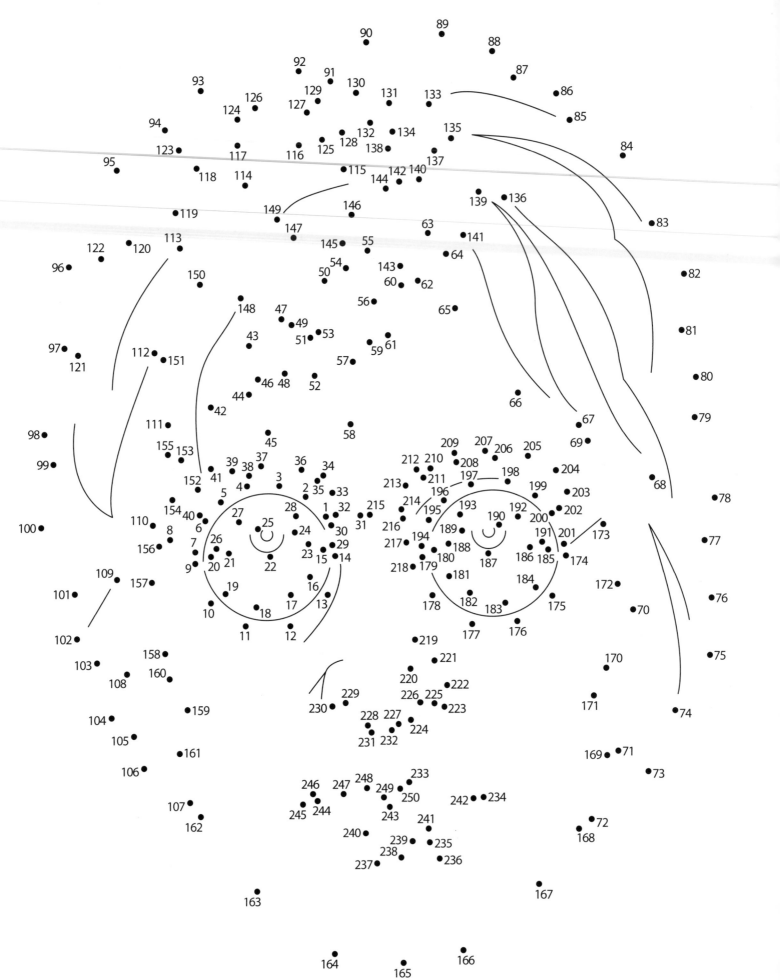

12

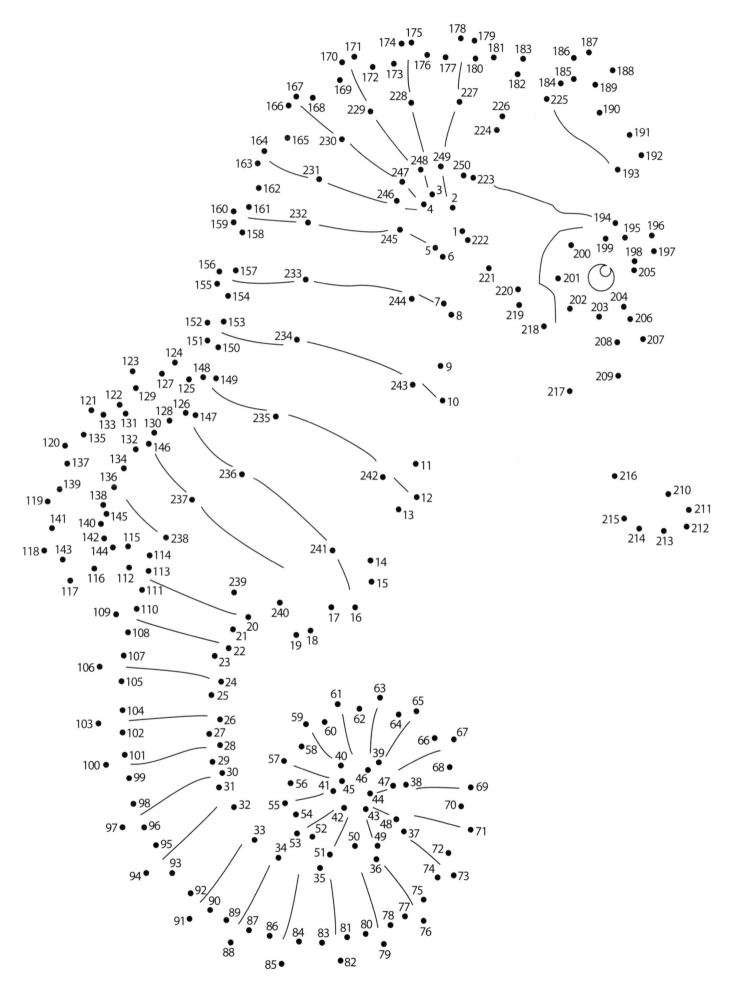

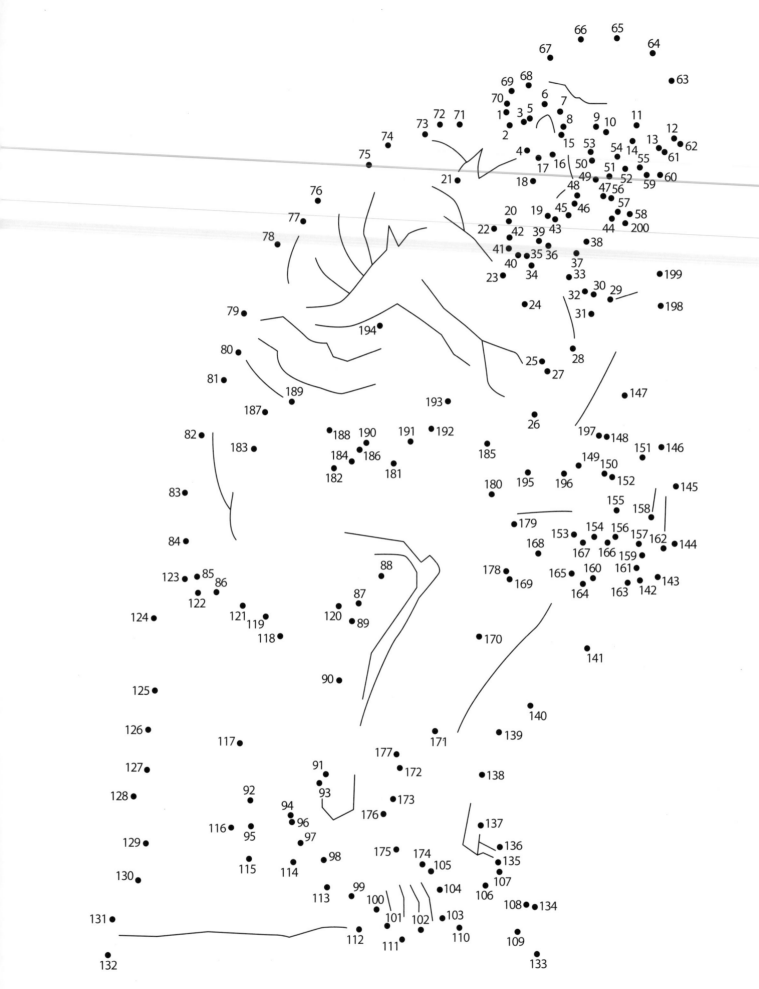

14

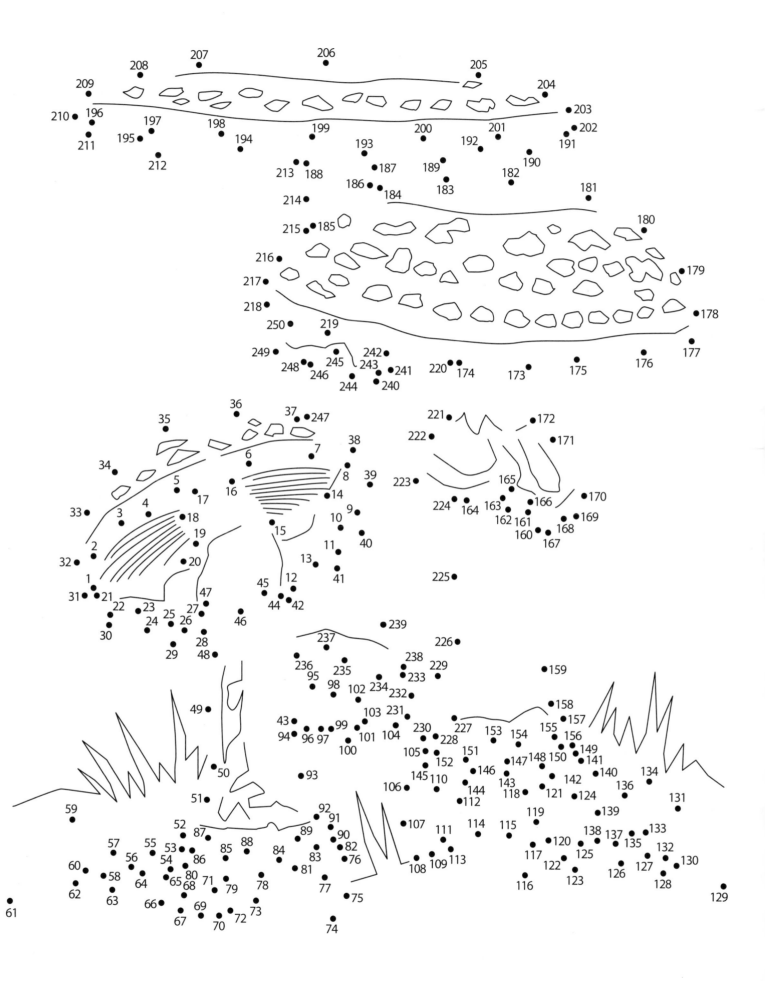

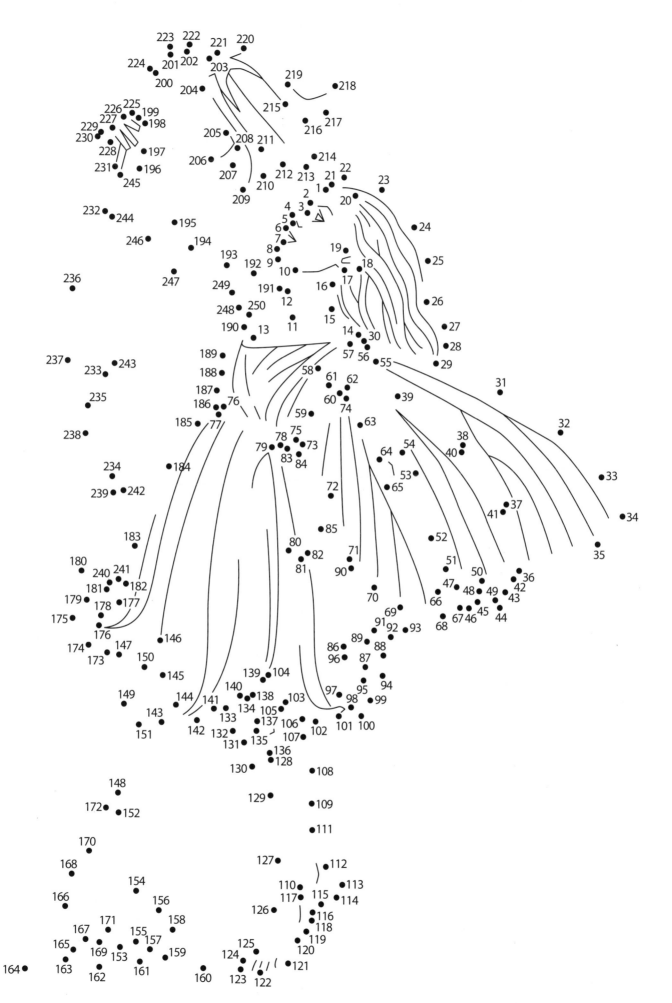

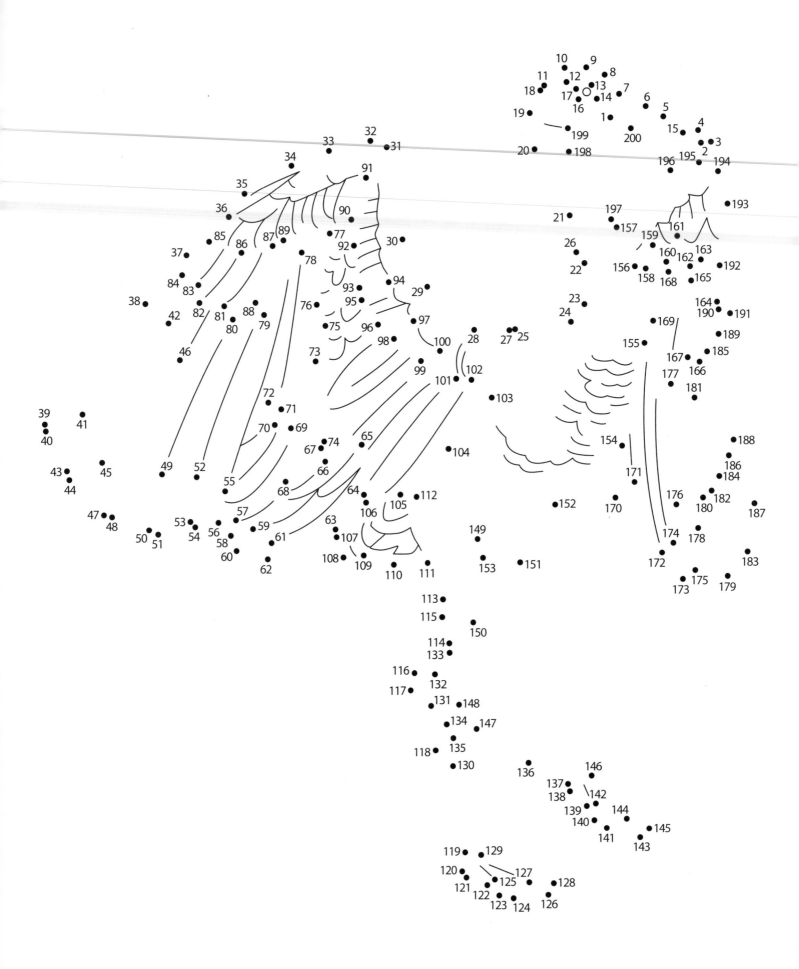

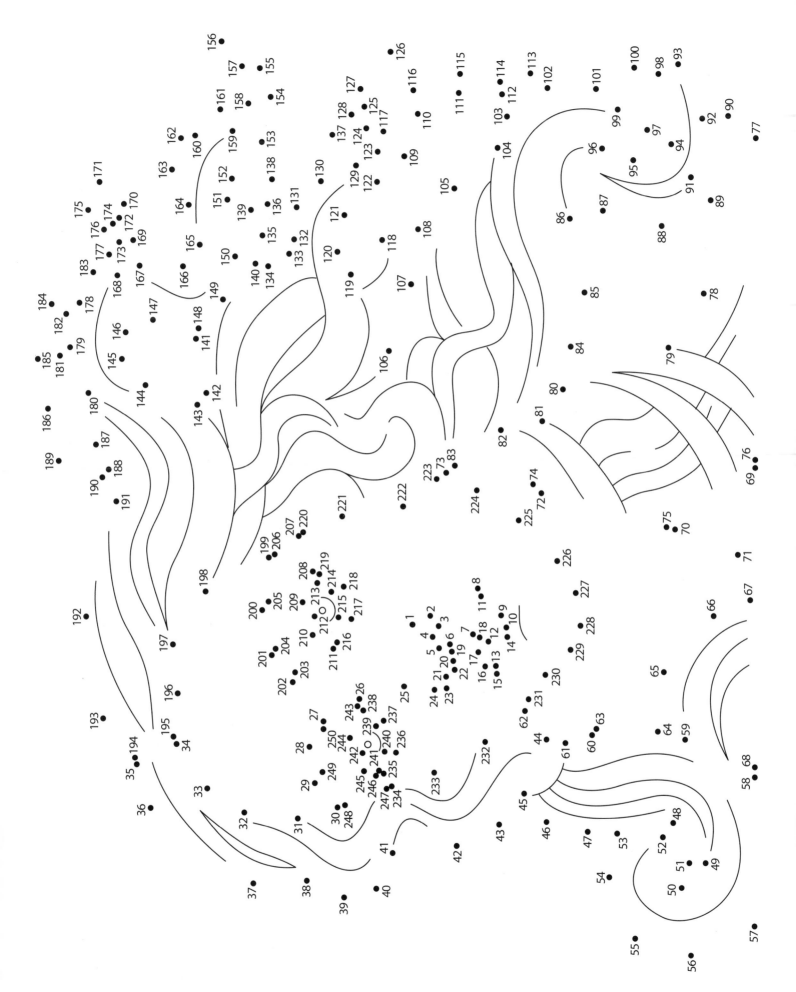

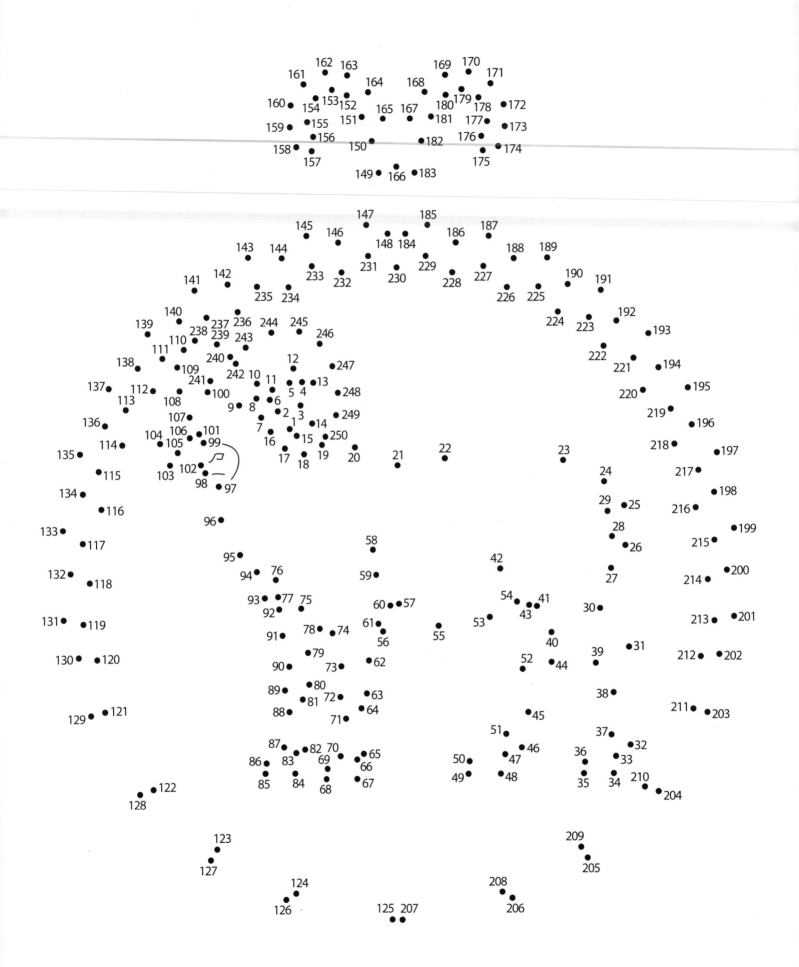

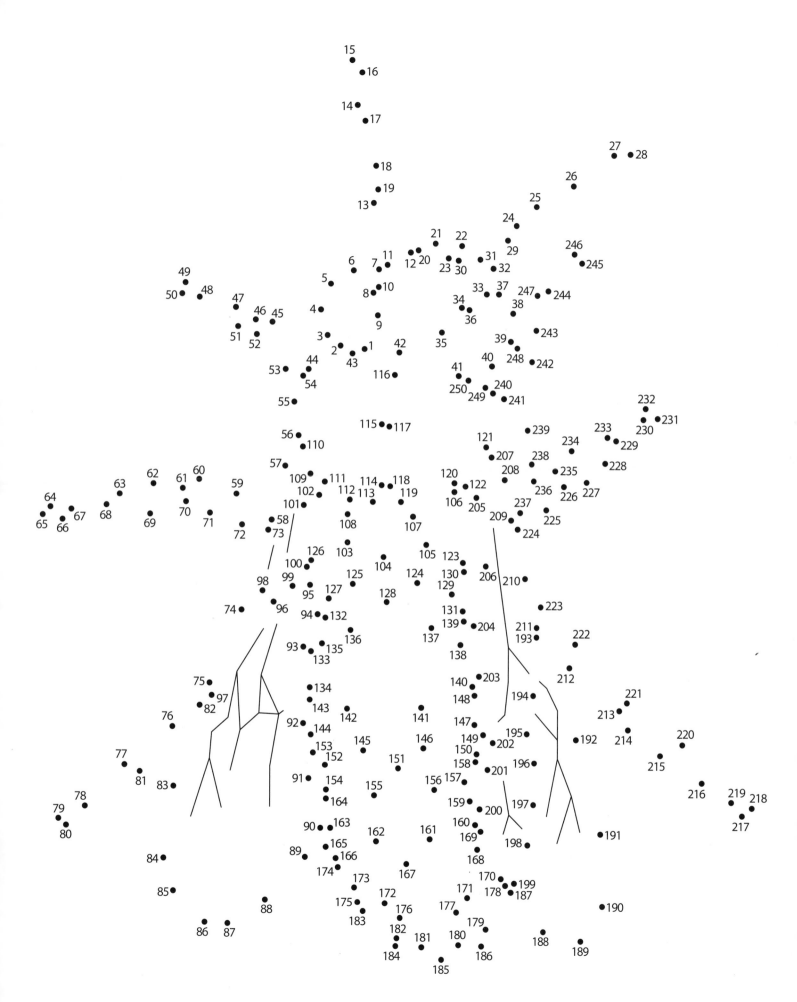

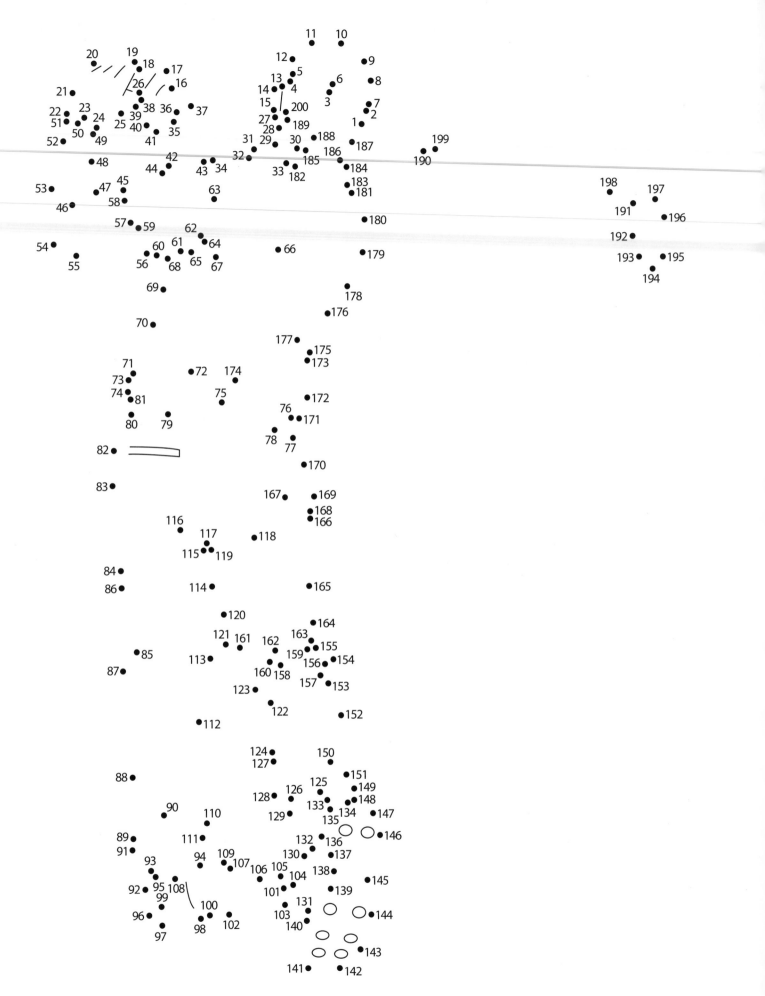

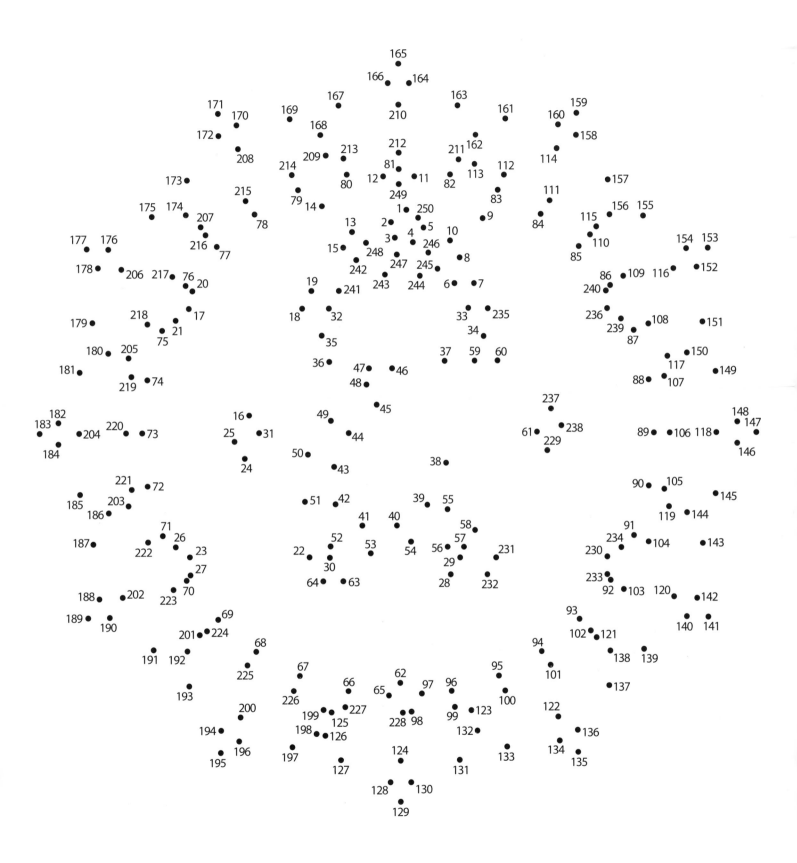

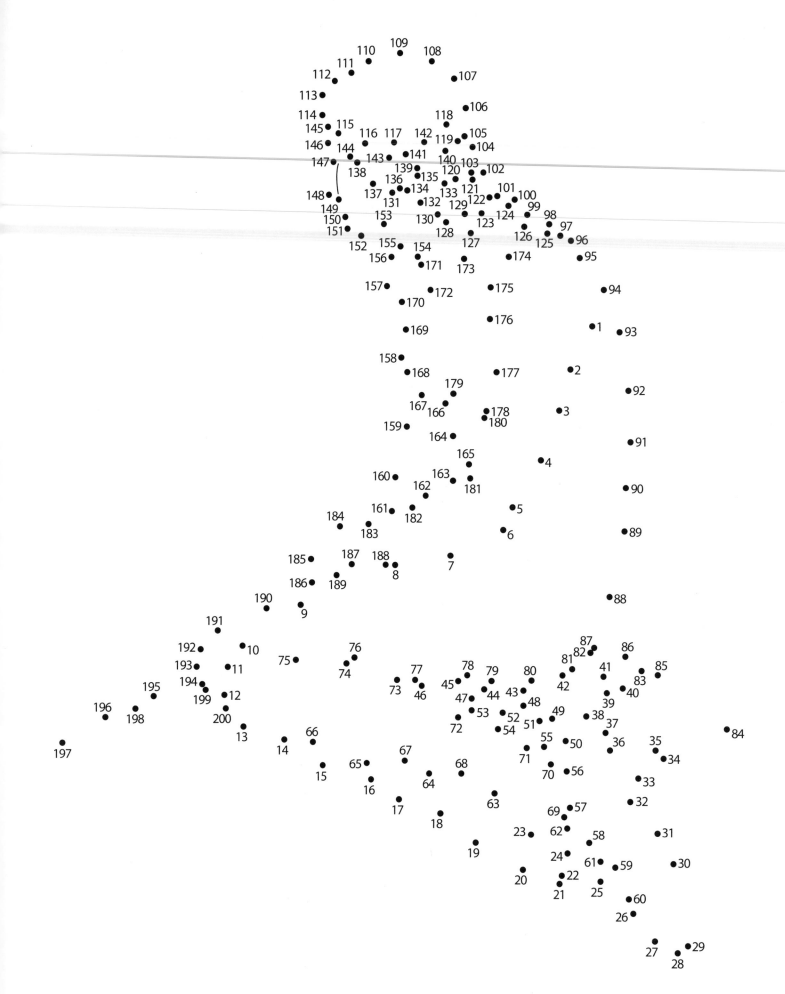

24

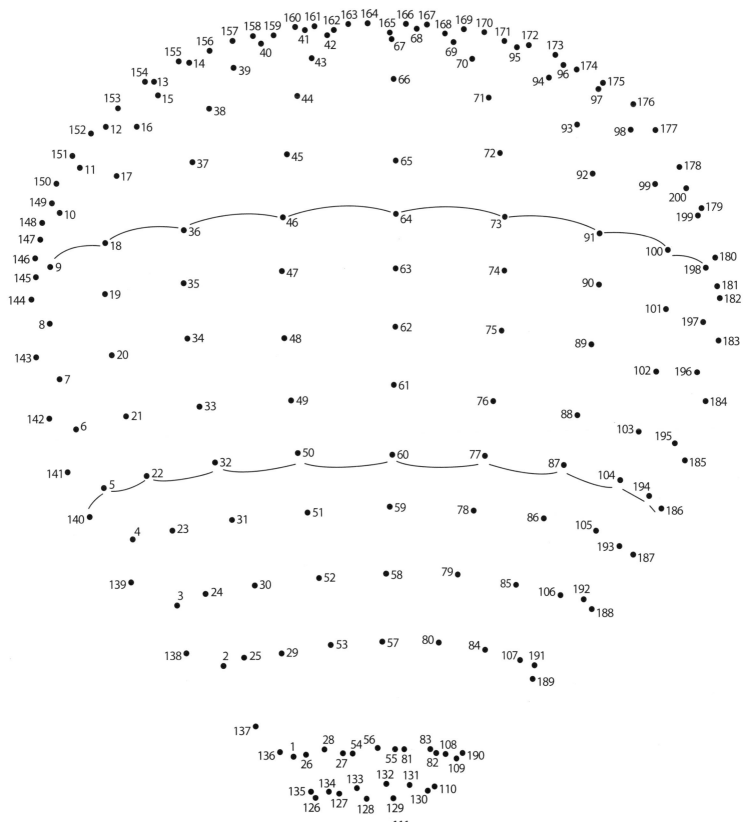
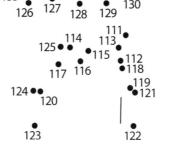

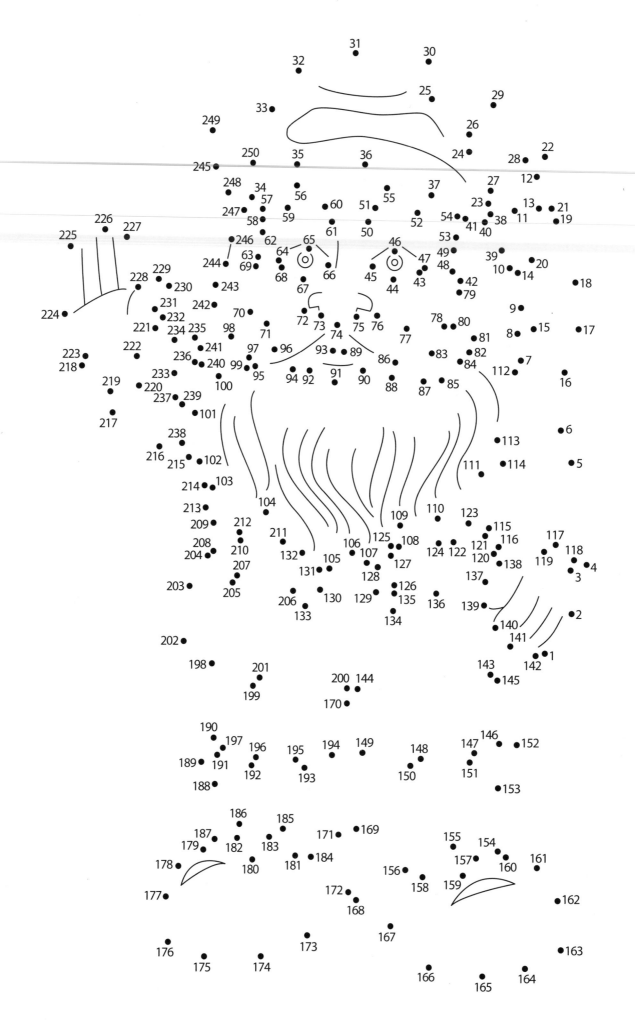

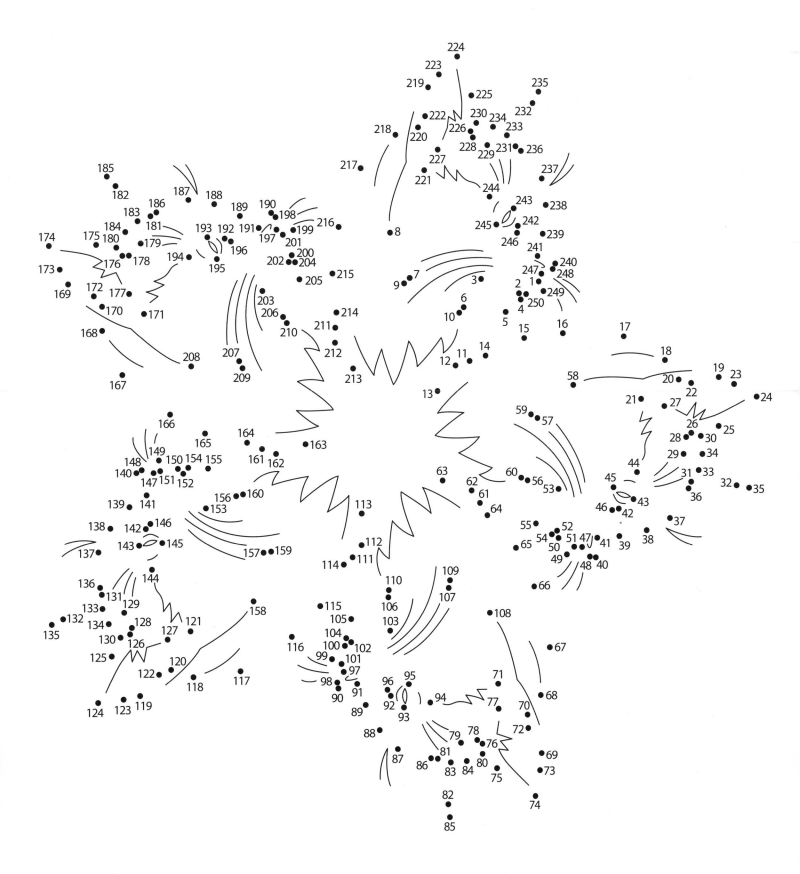

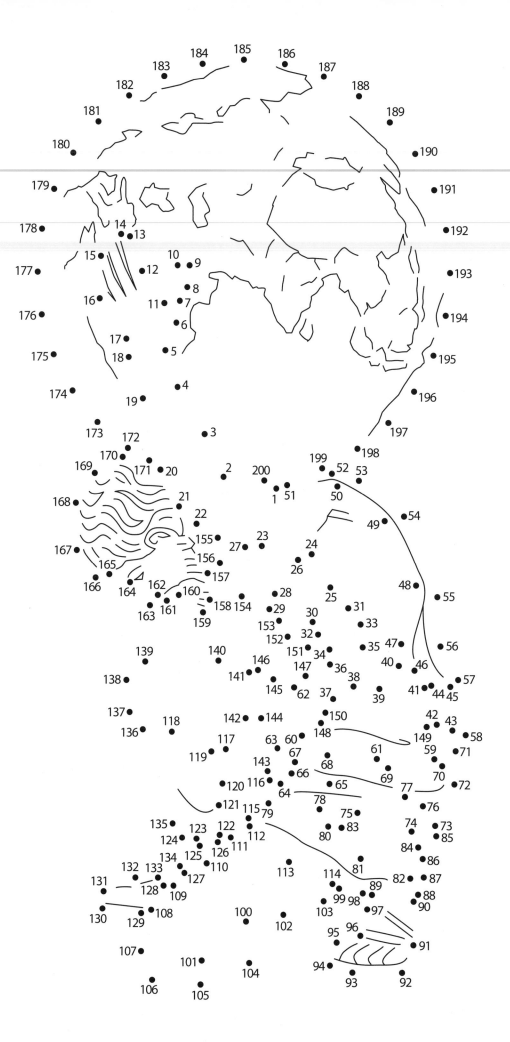

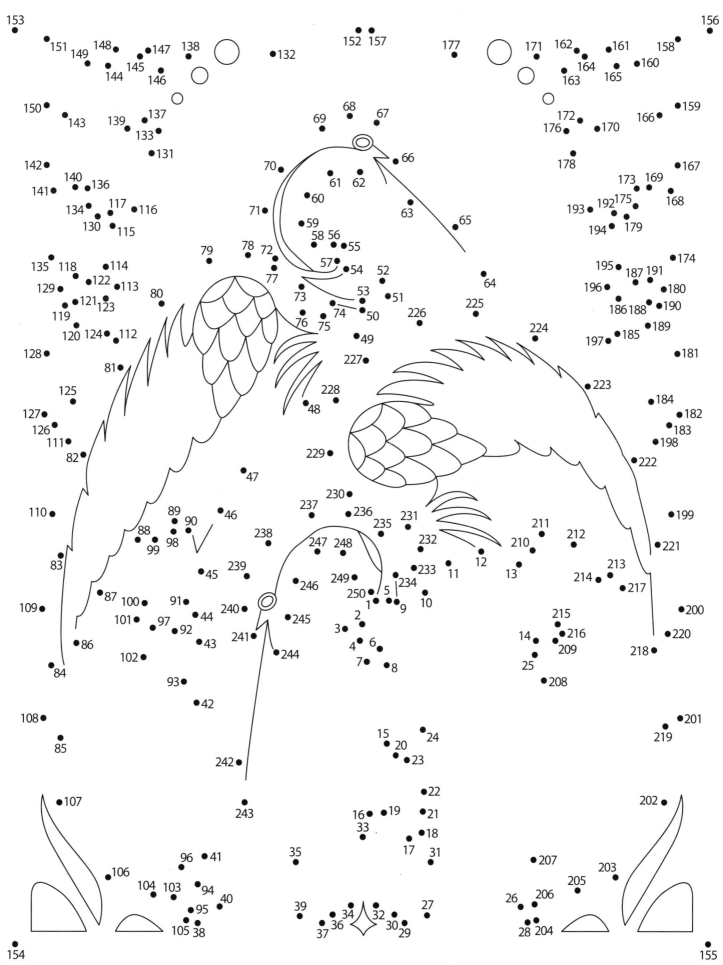

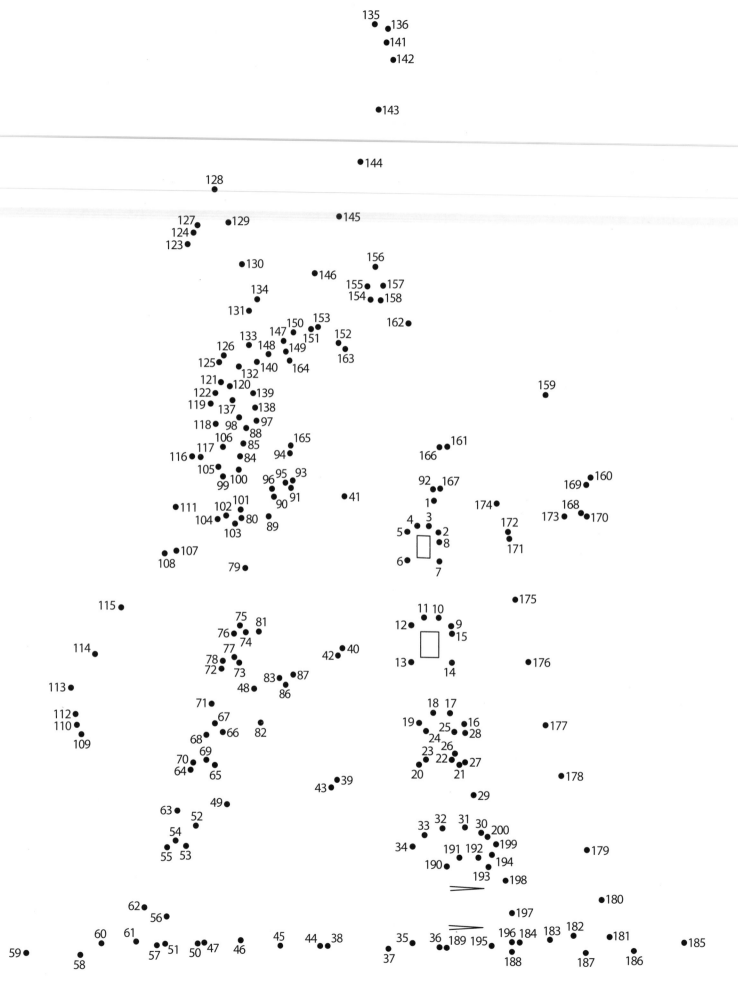

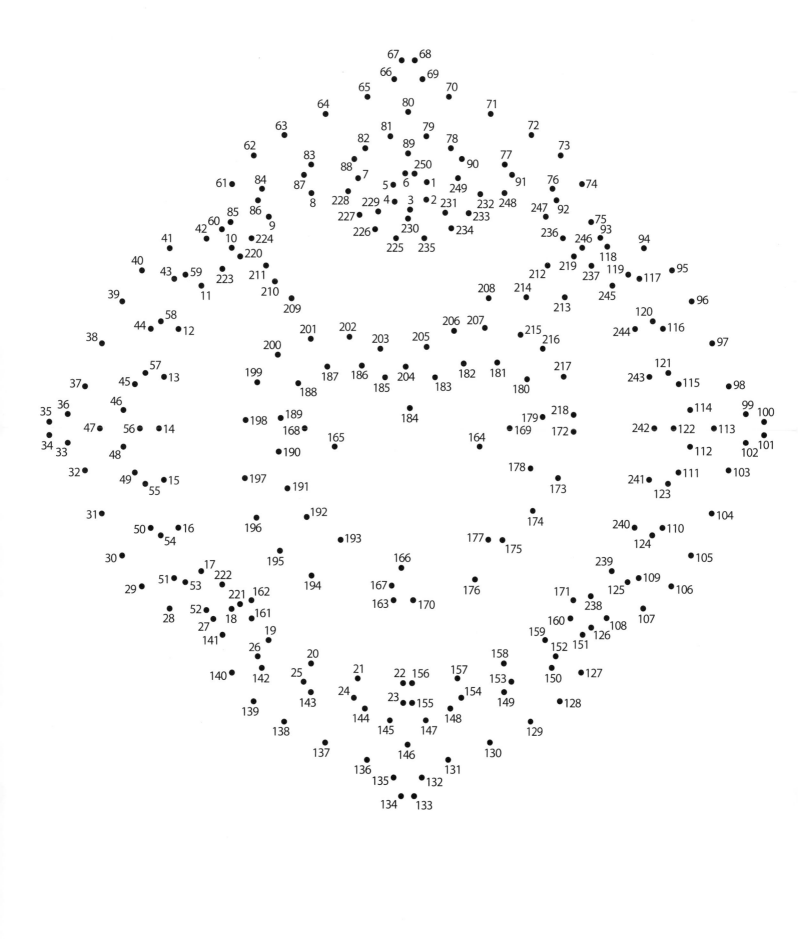

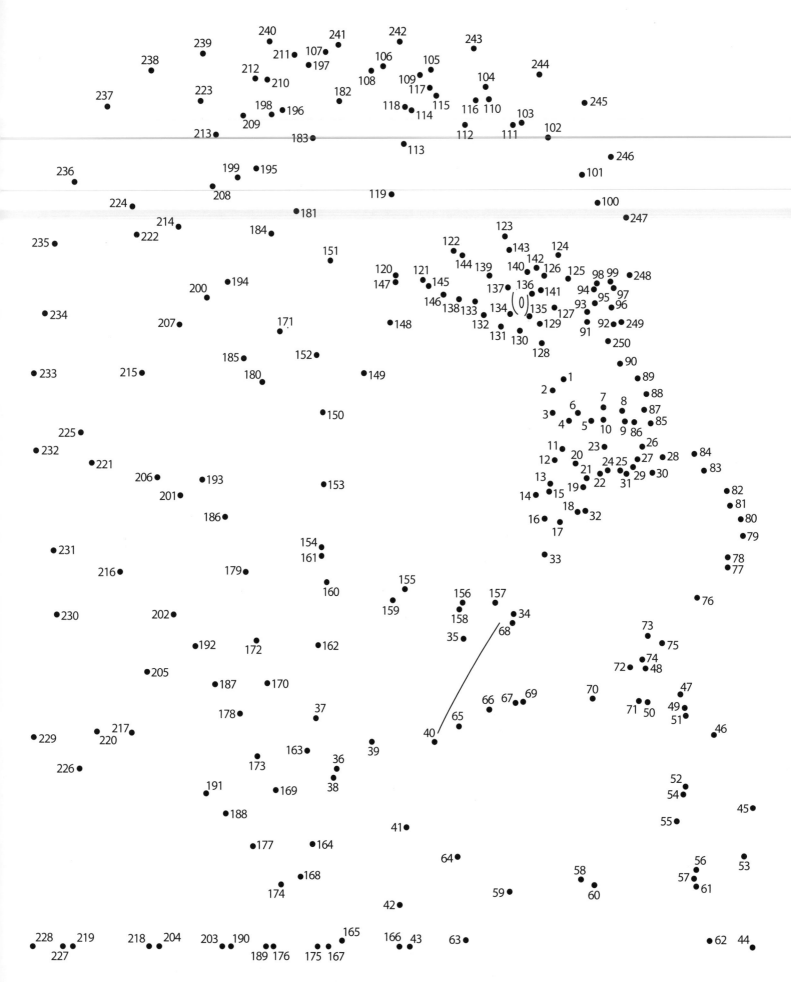

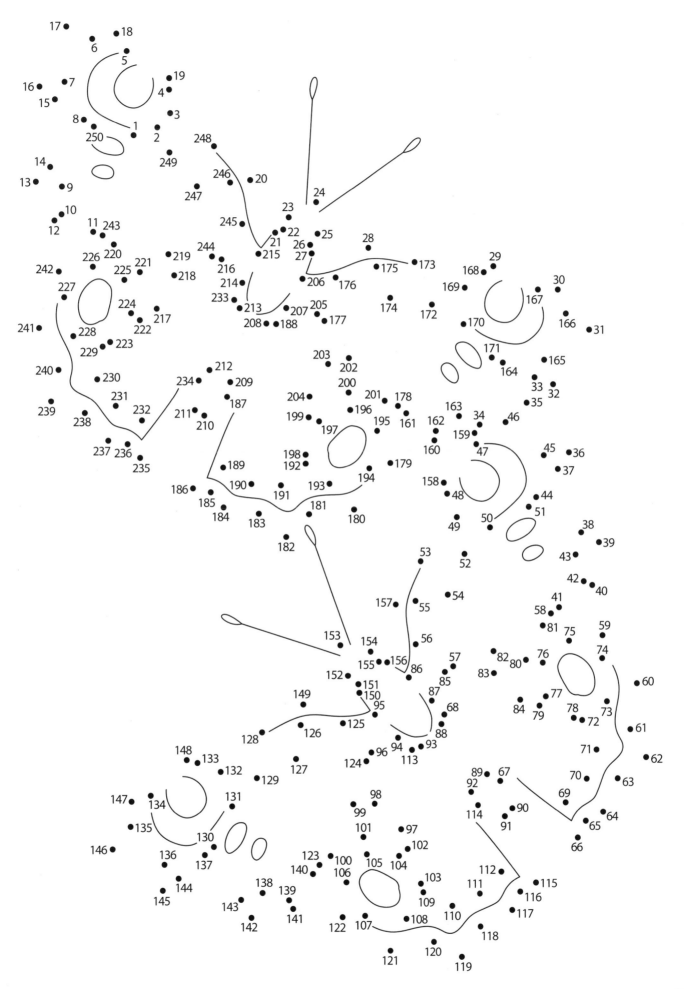

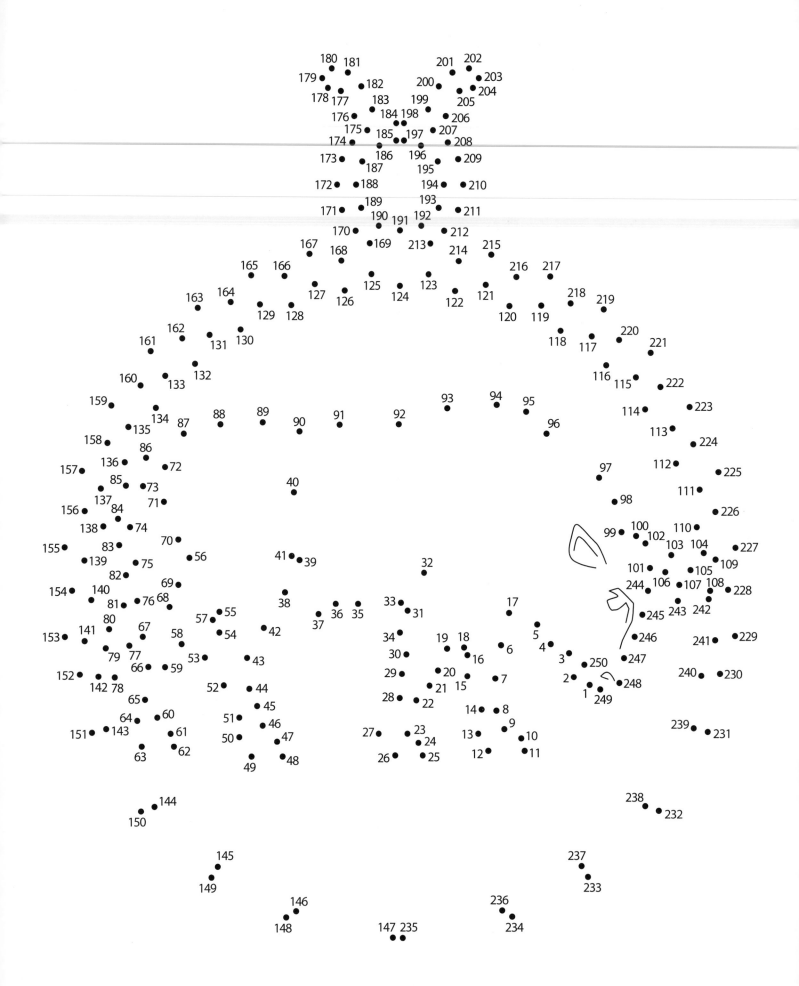

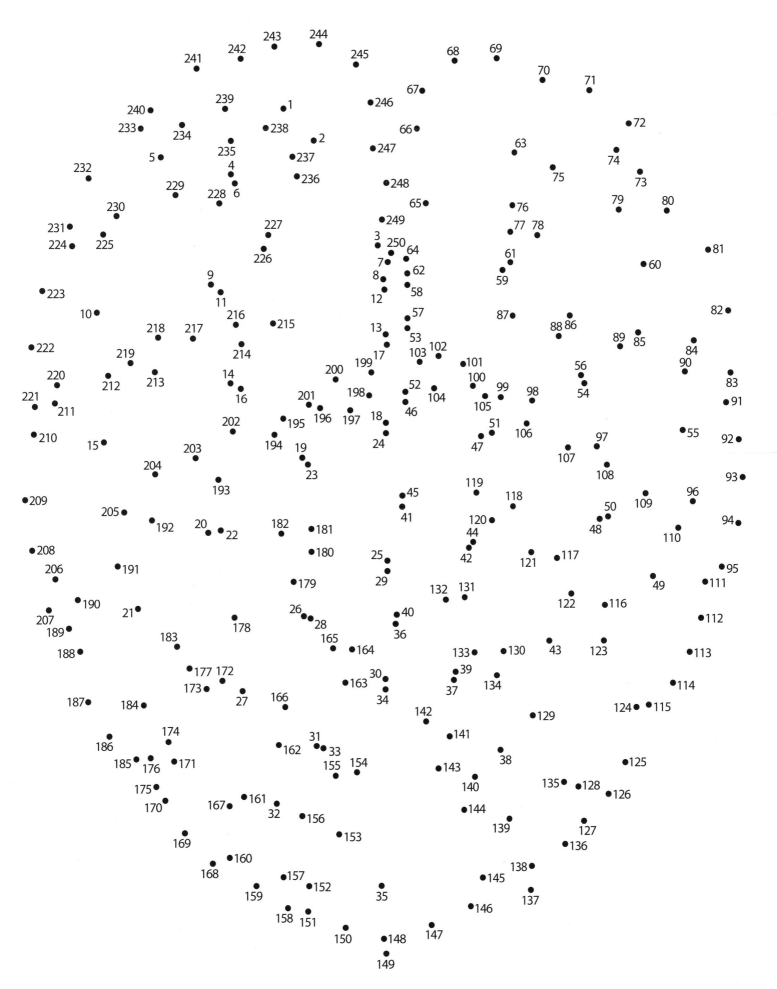

35

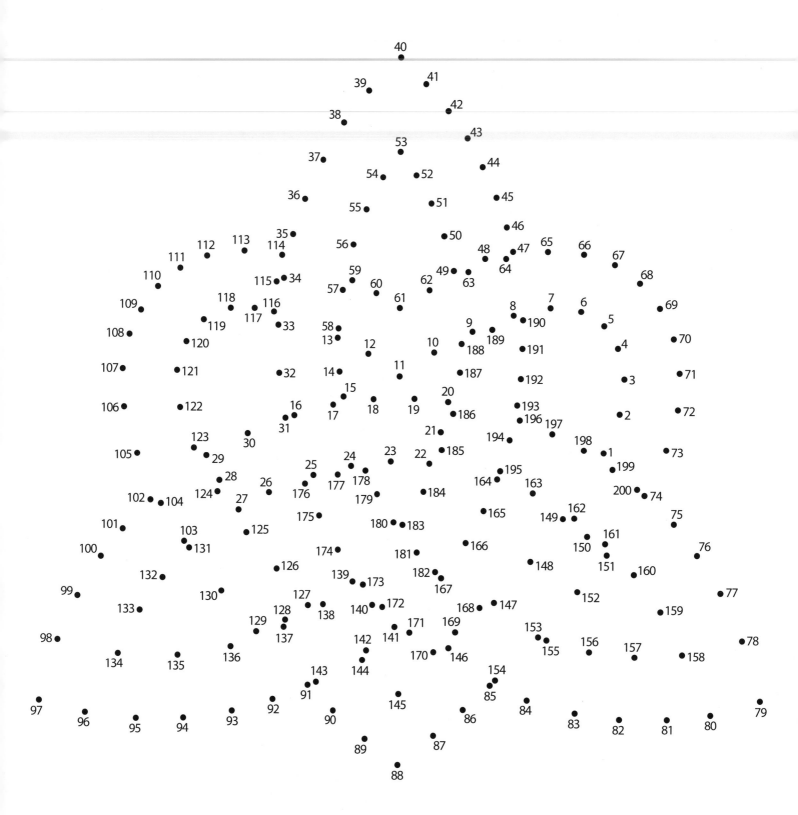

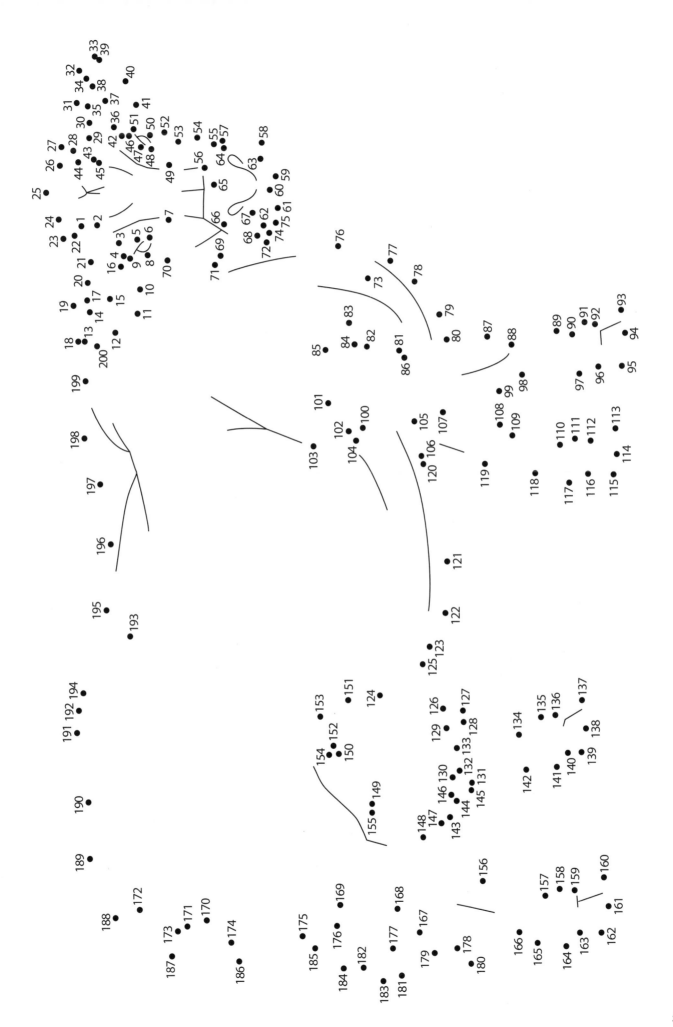

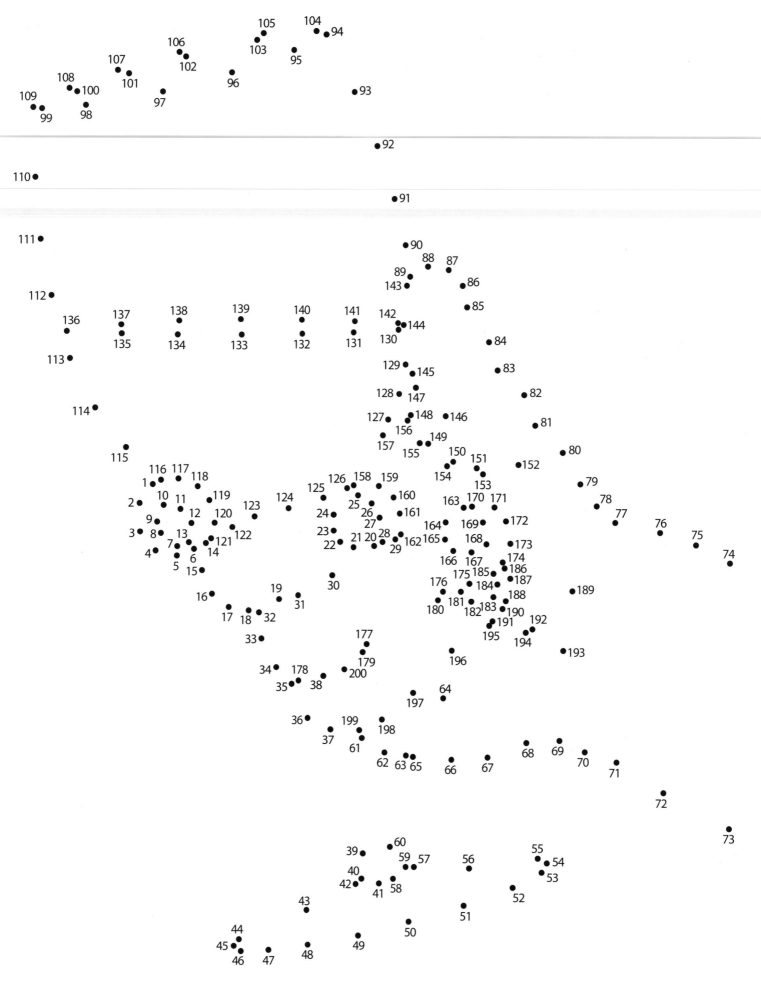

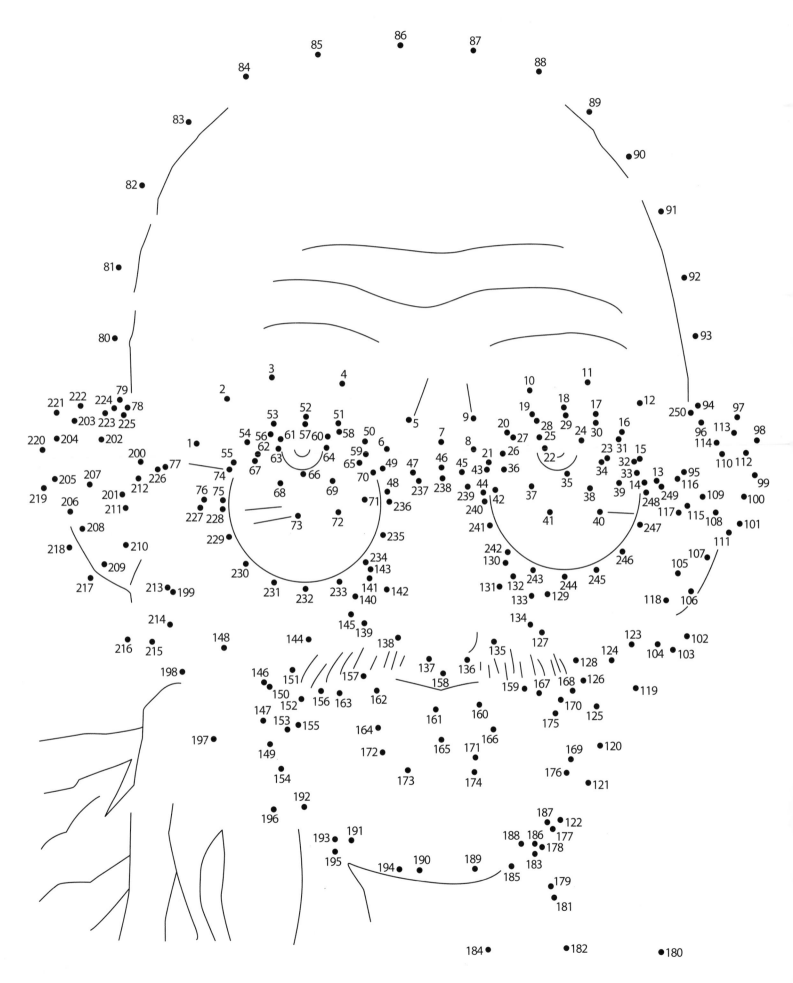

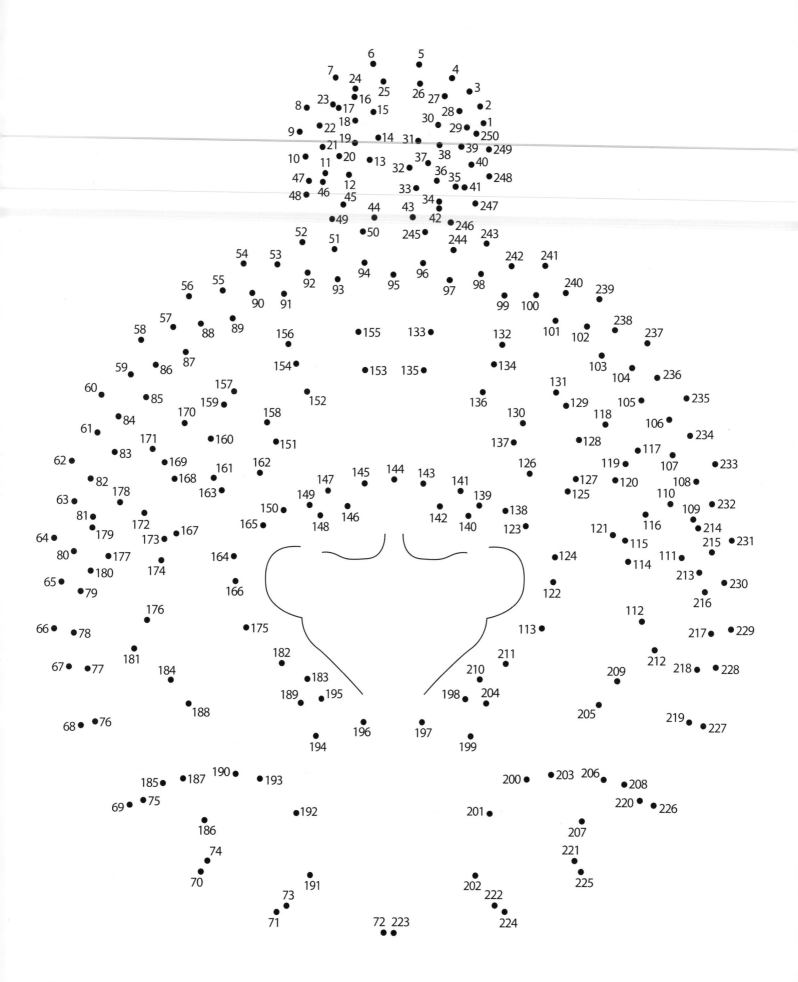

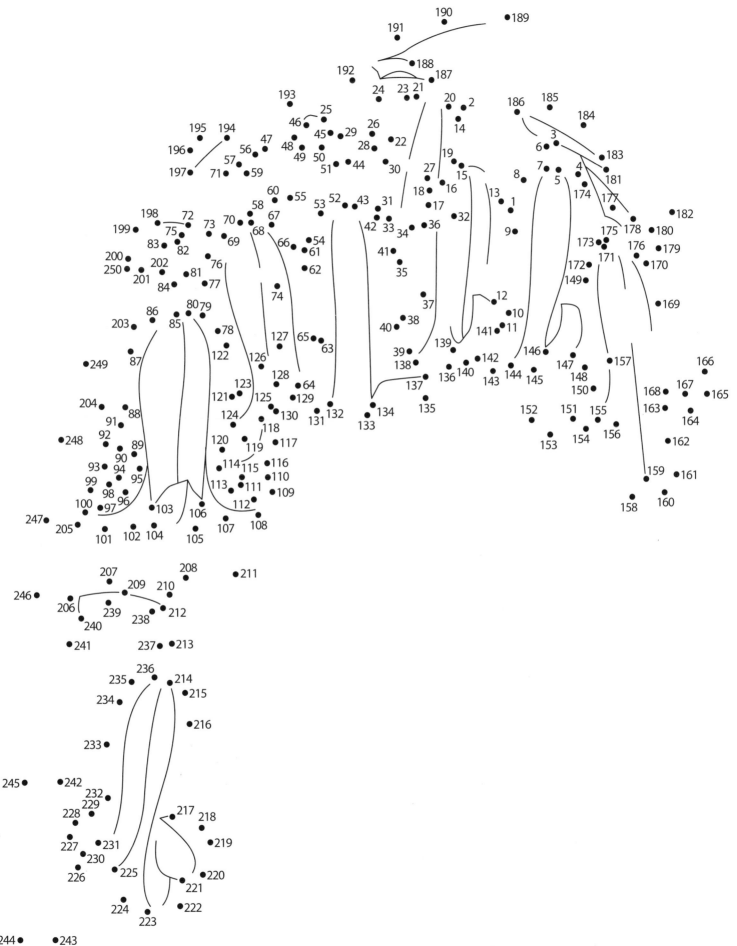

41

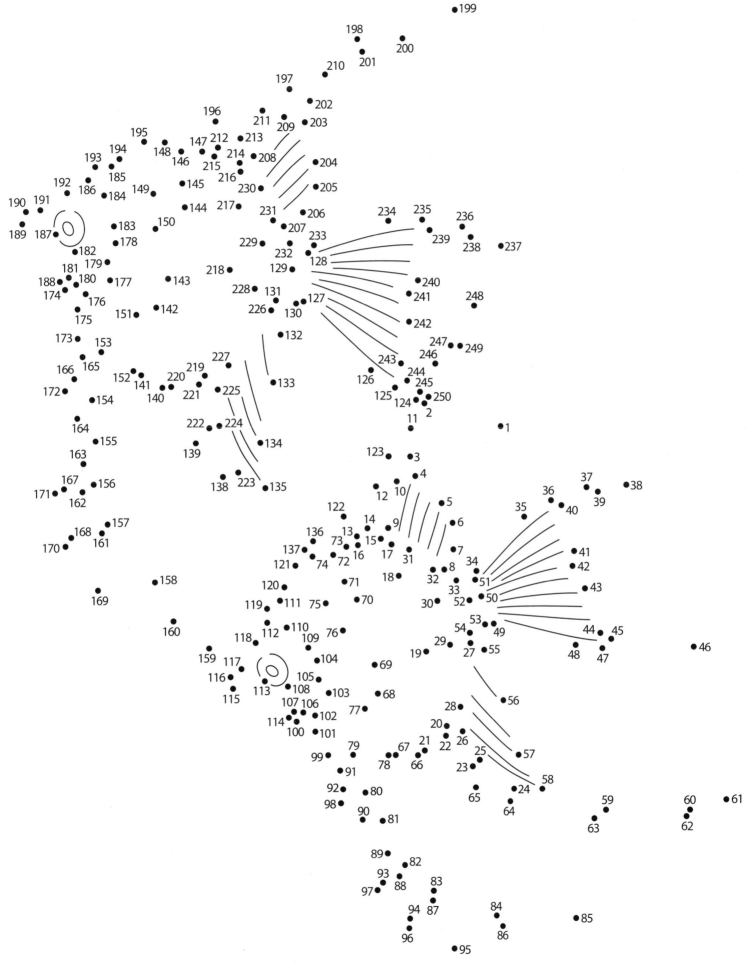

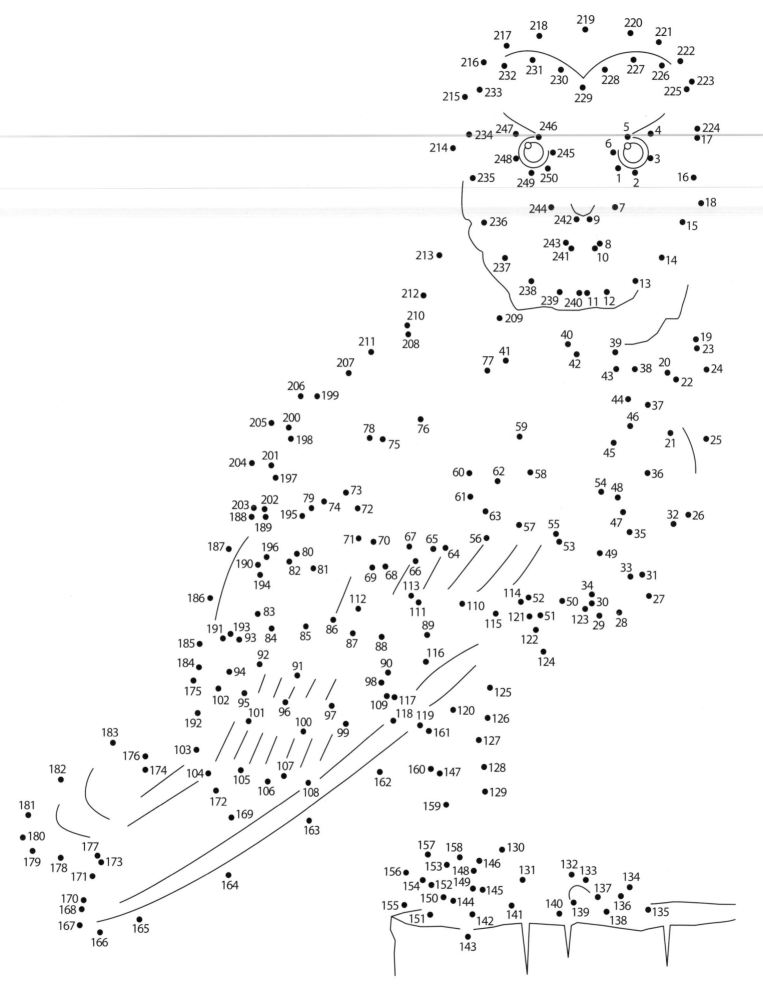

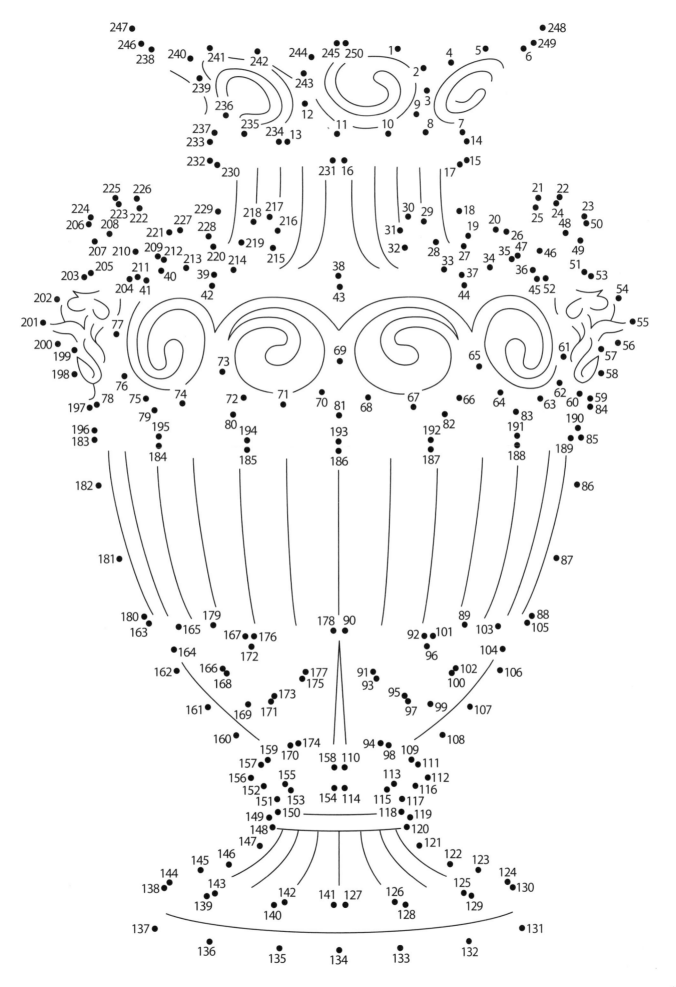

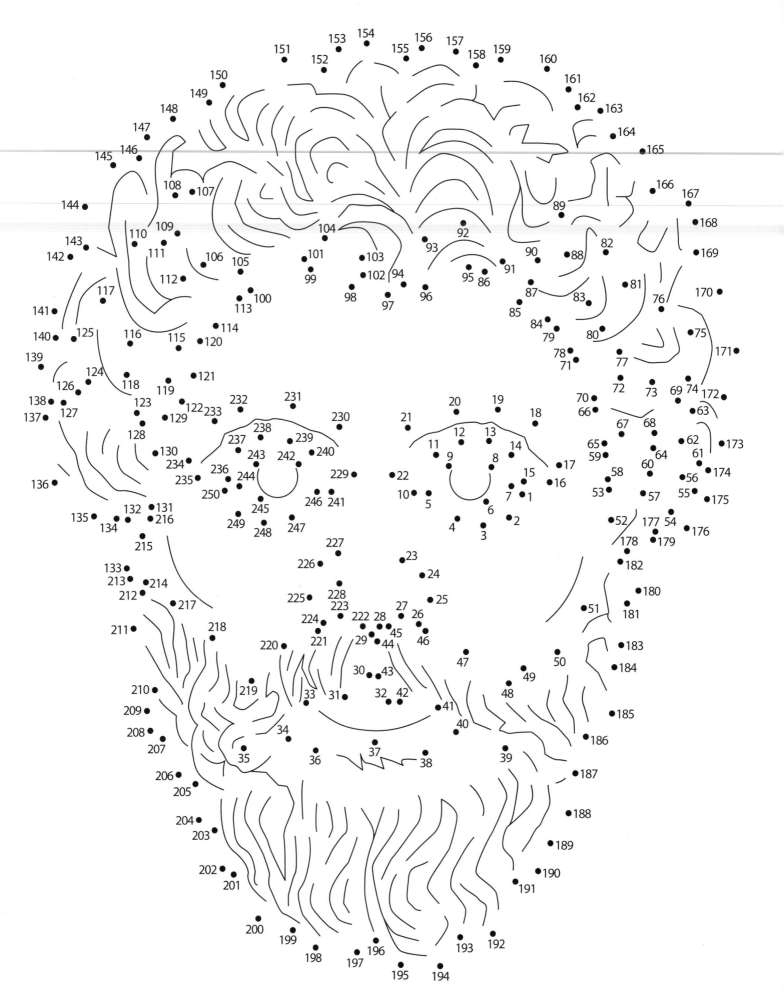

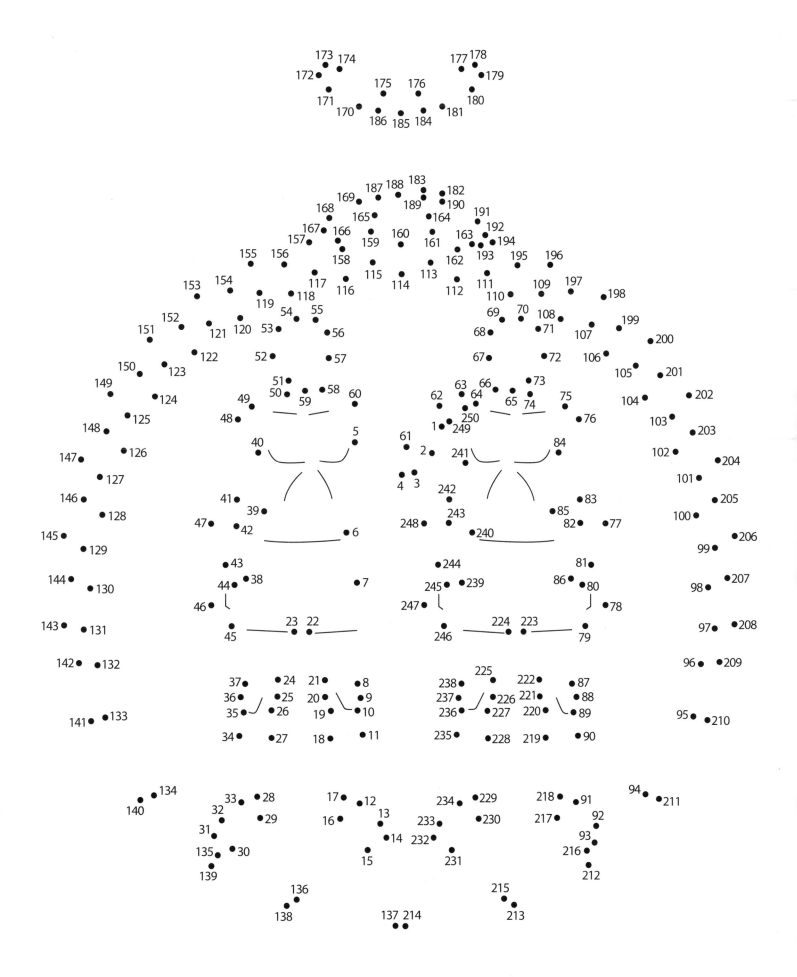

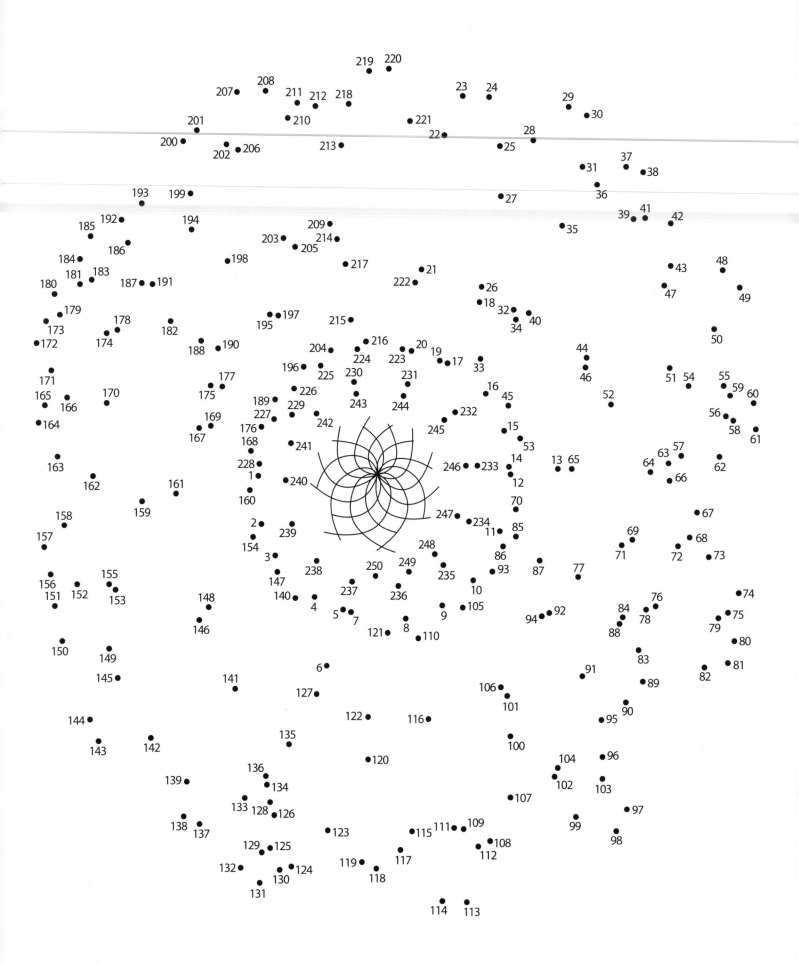

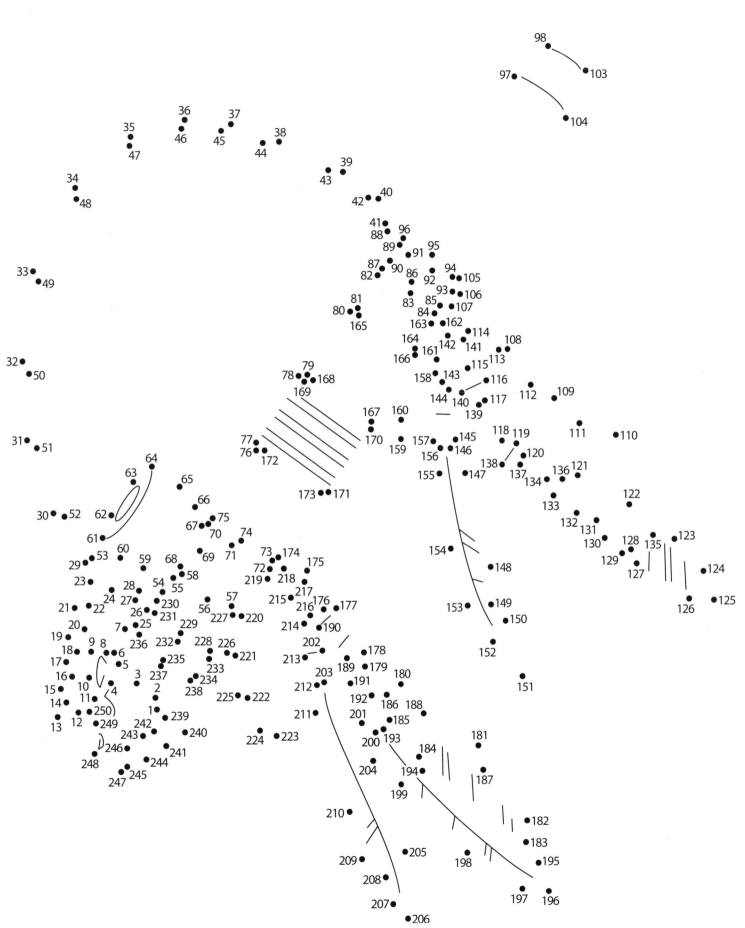

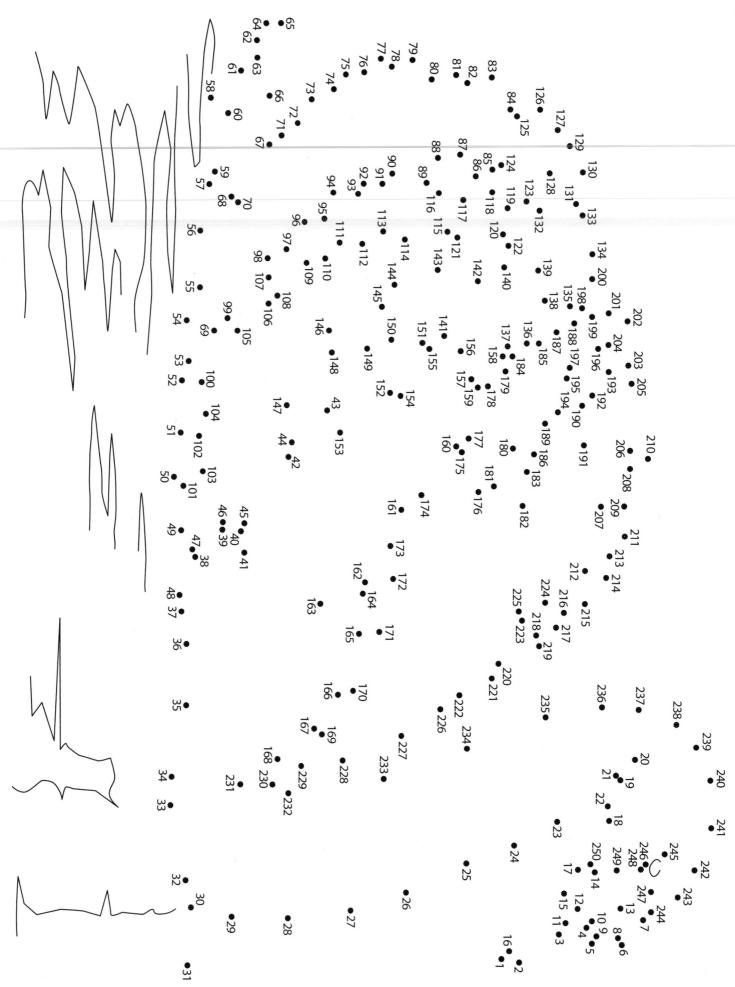

50

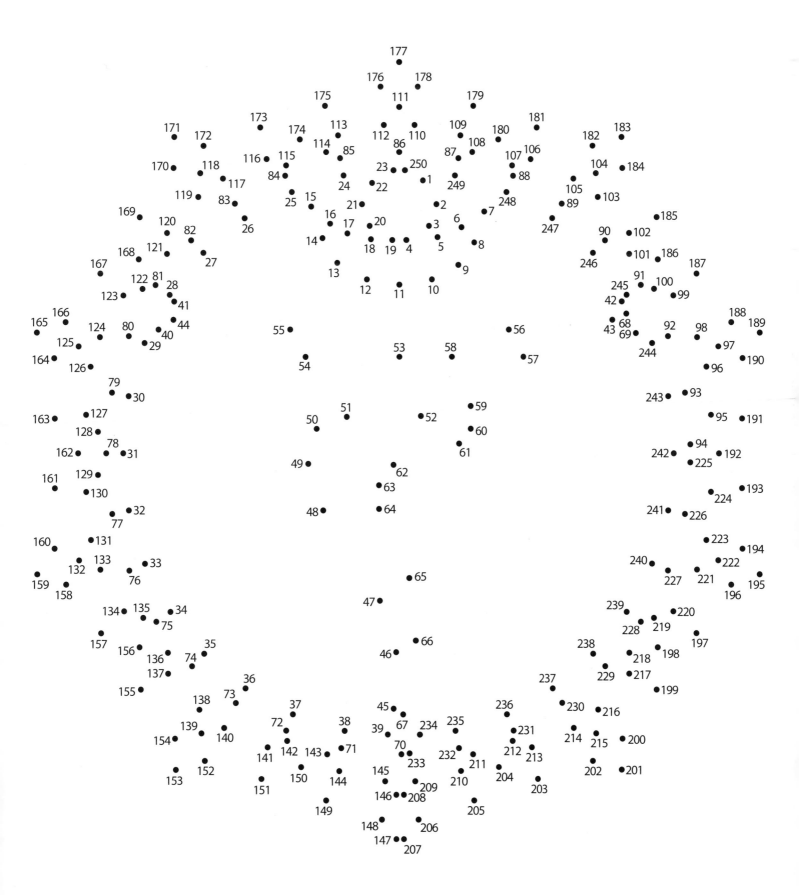

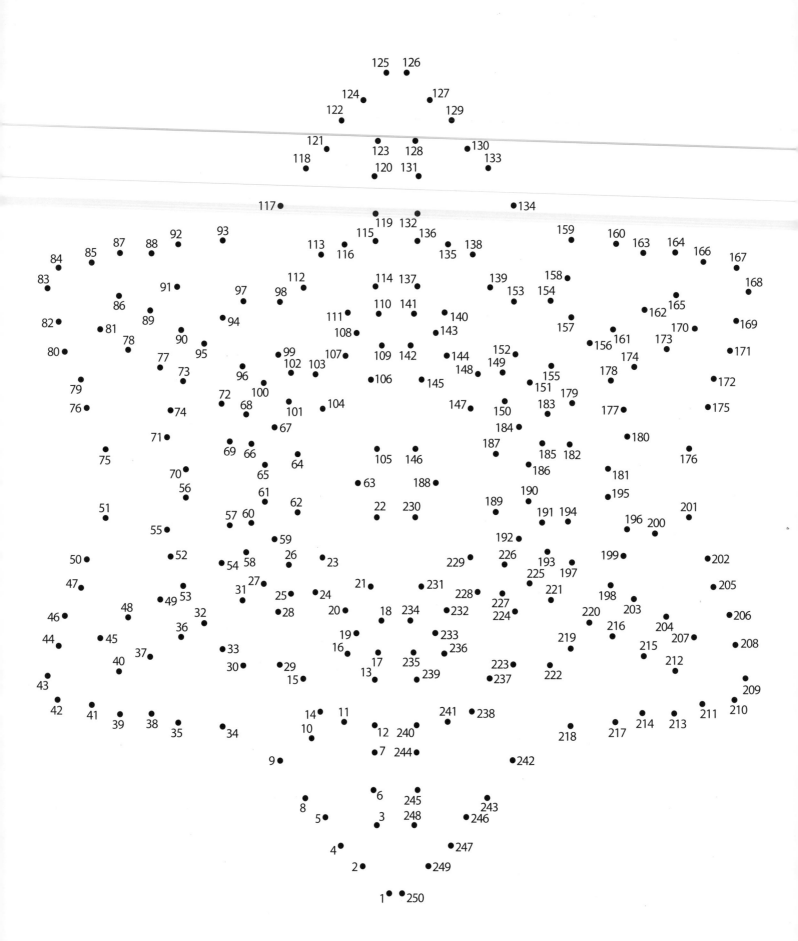

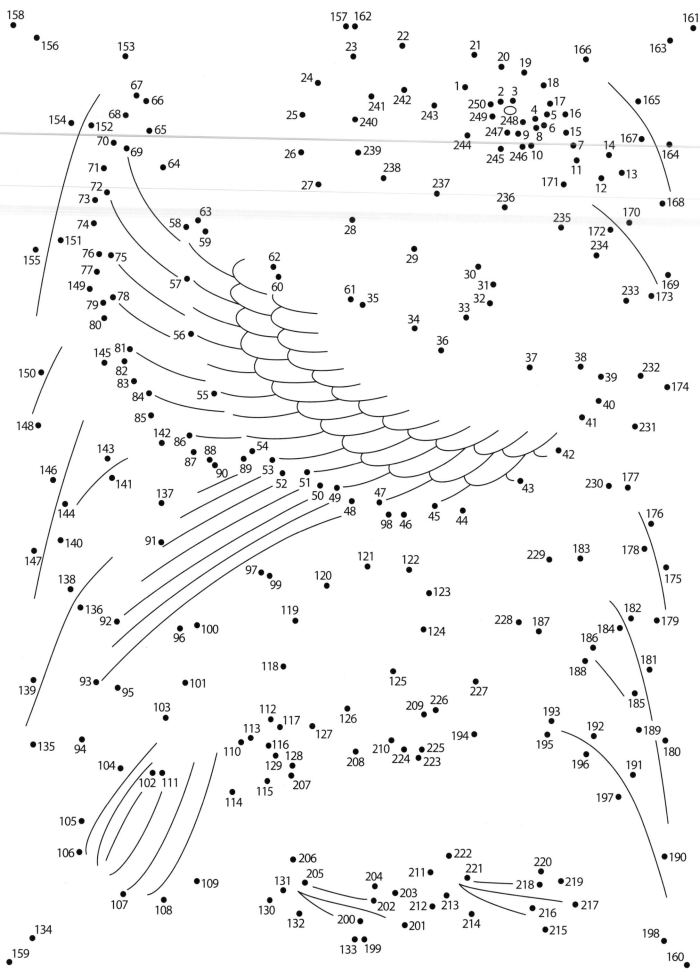

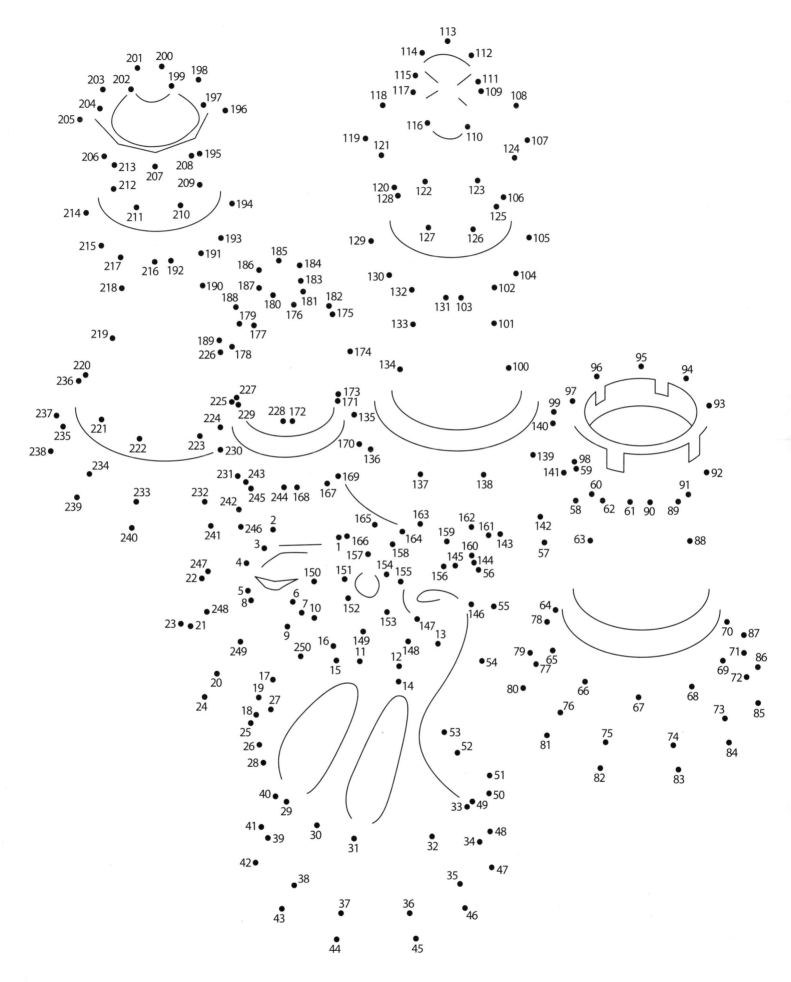

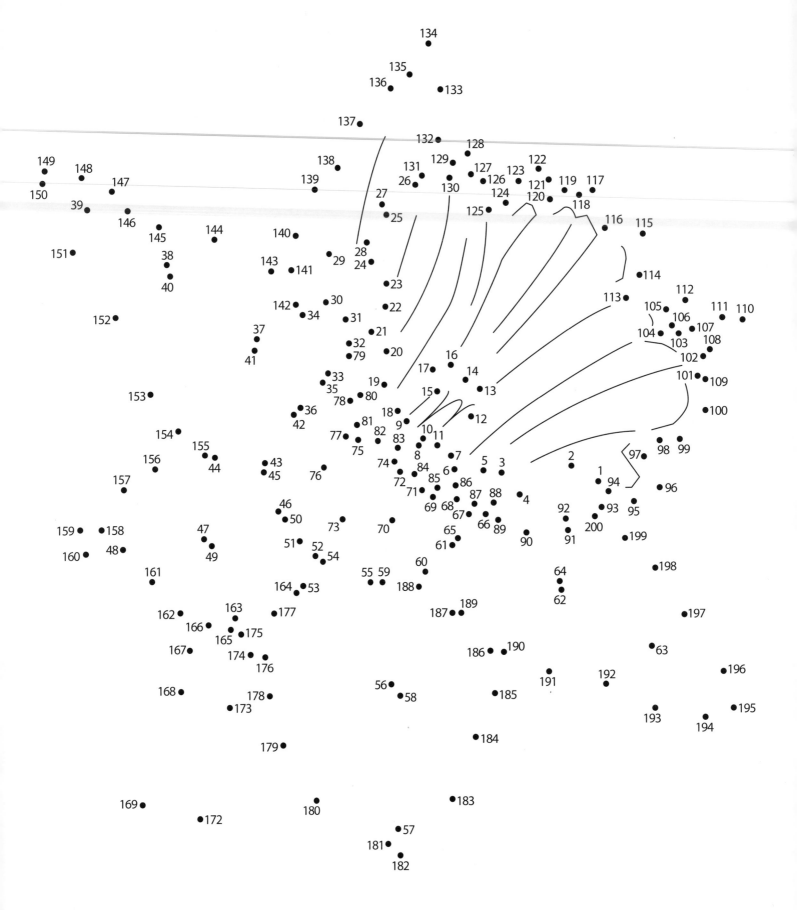

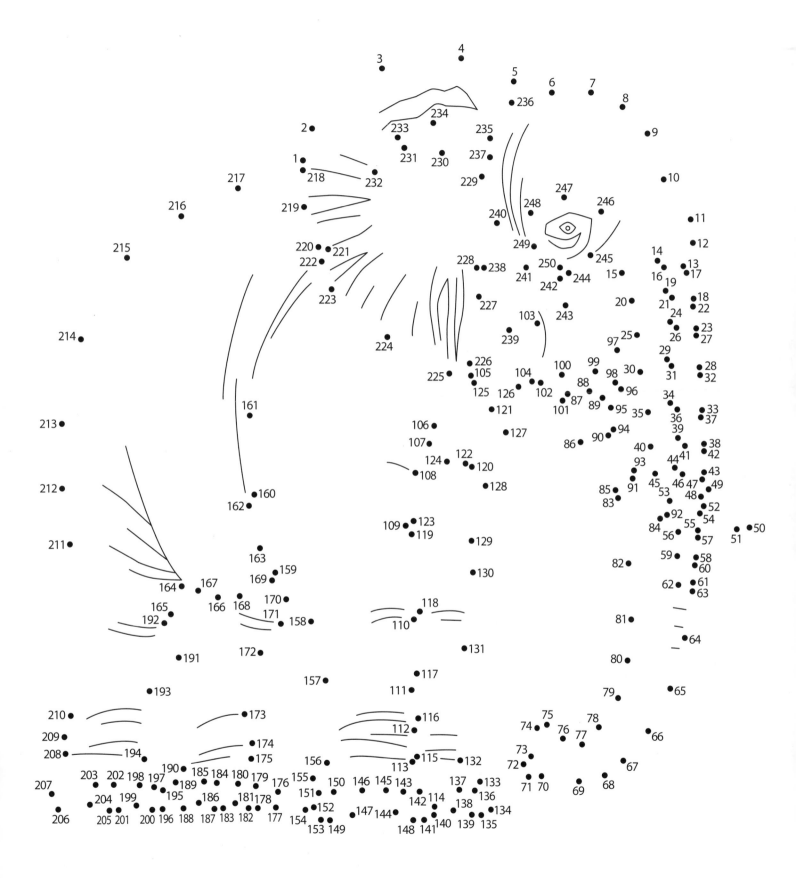

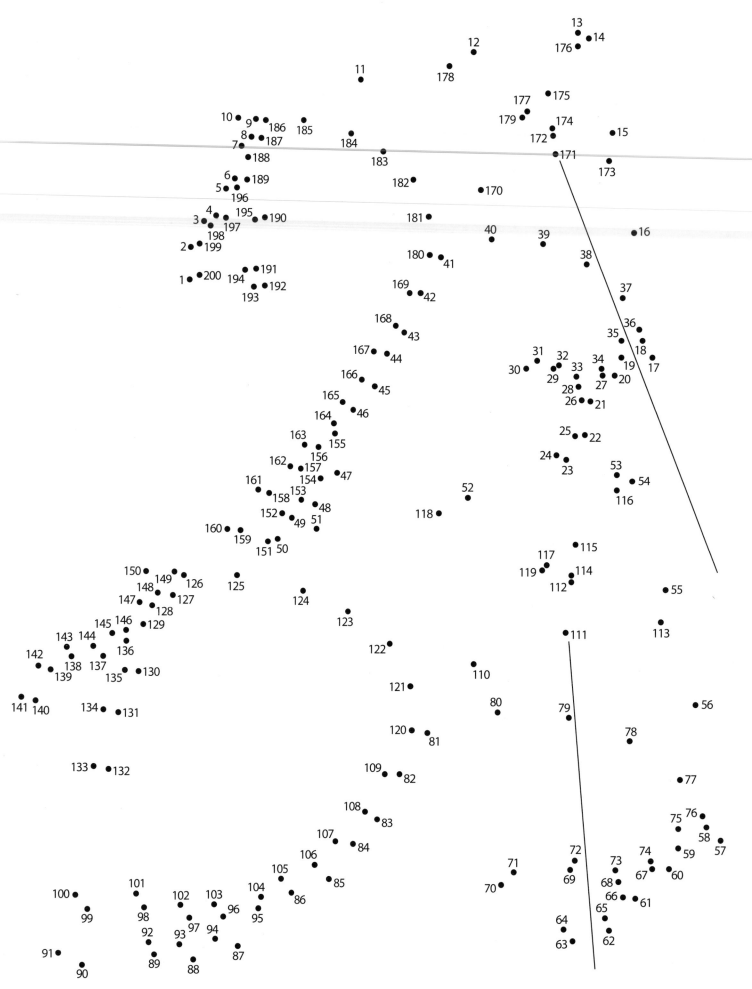

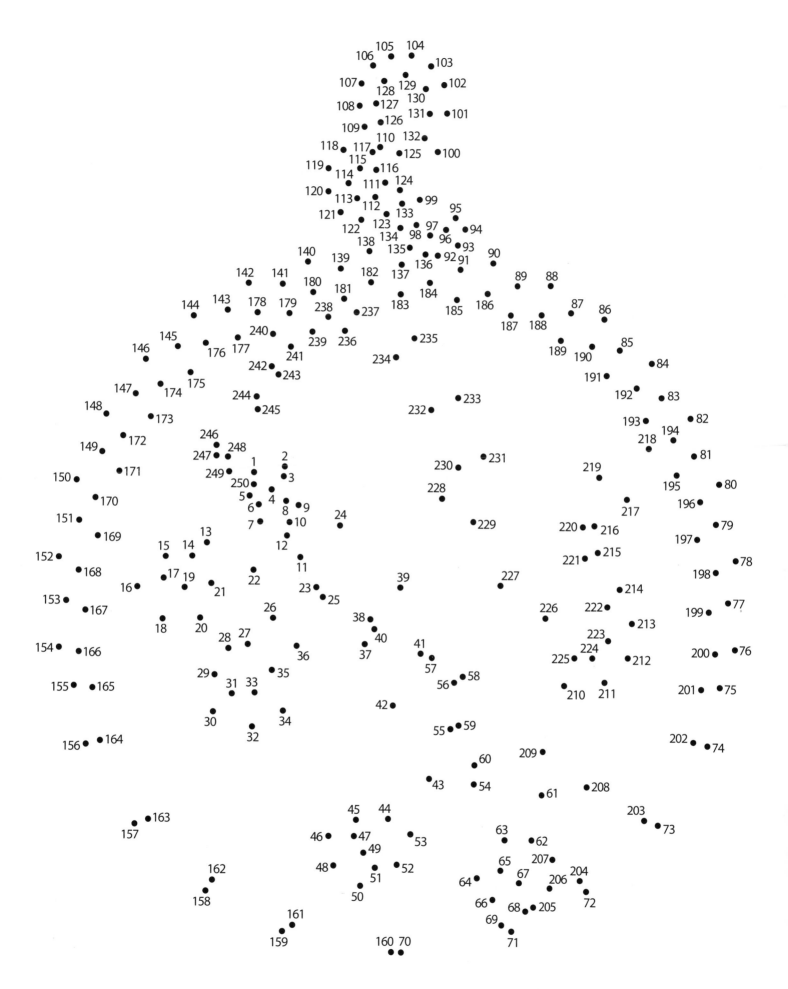

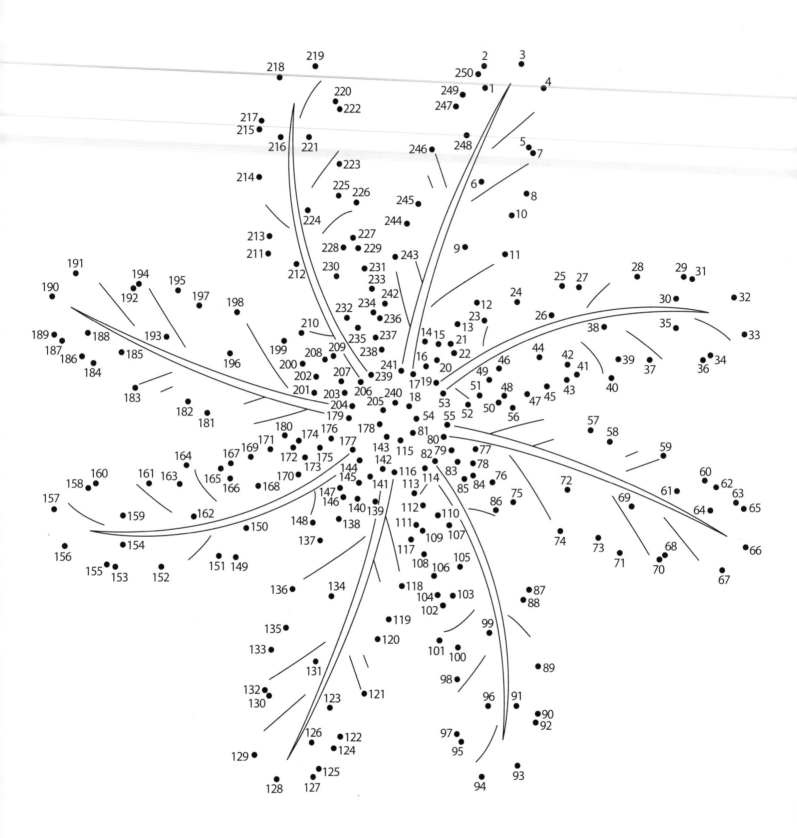

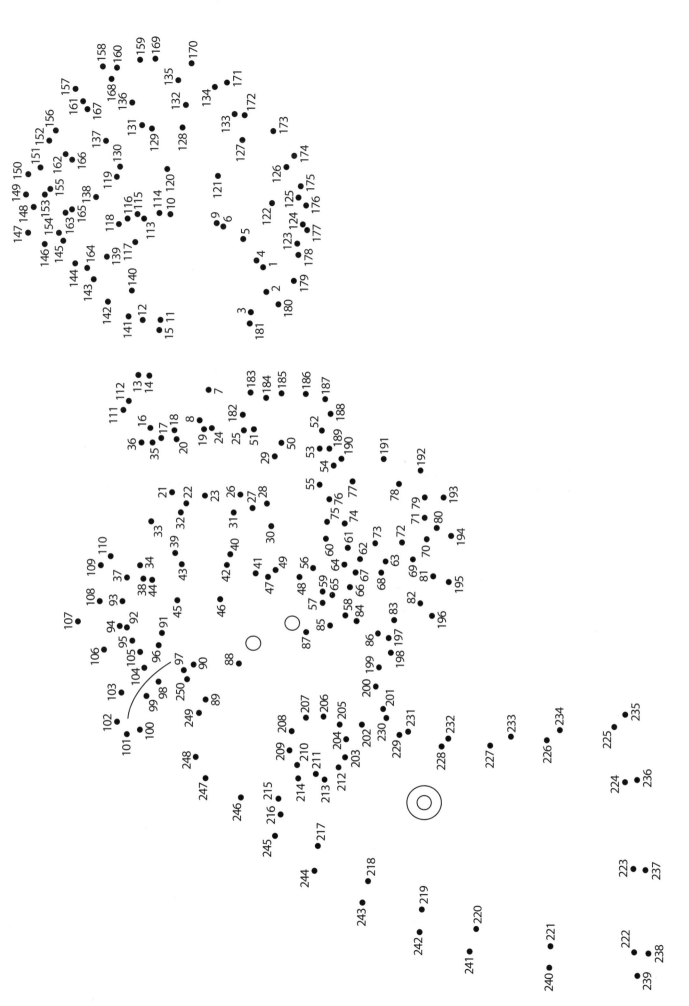

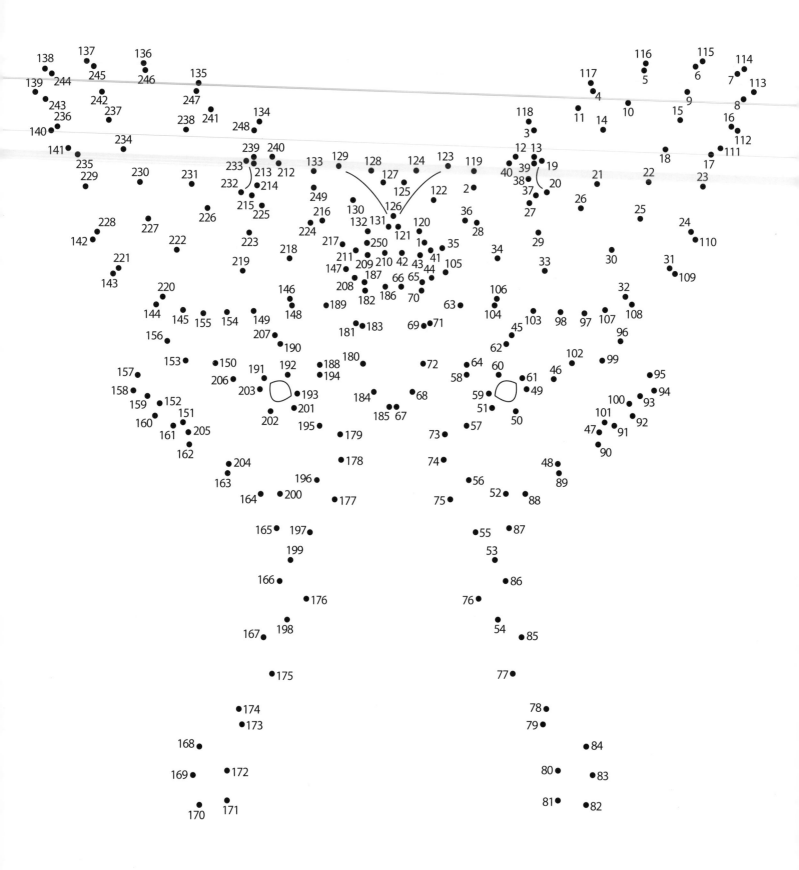

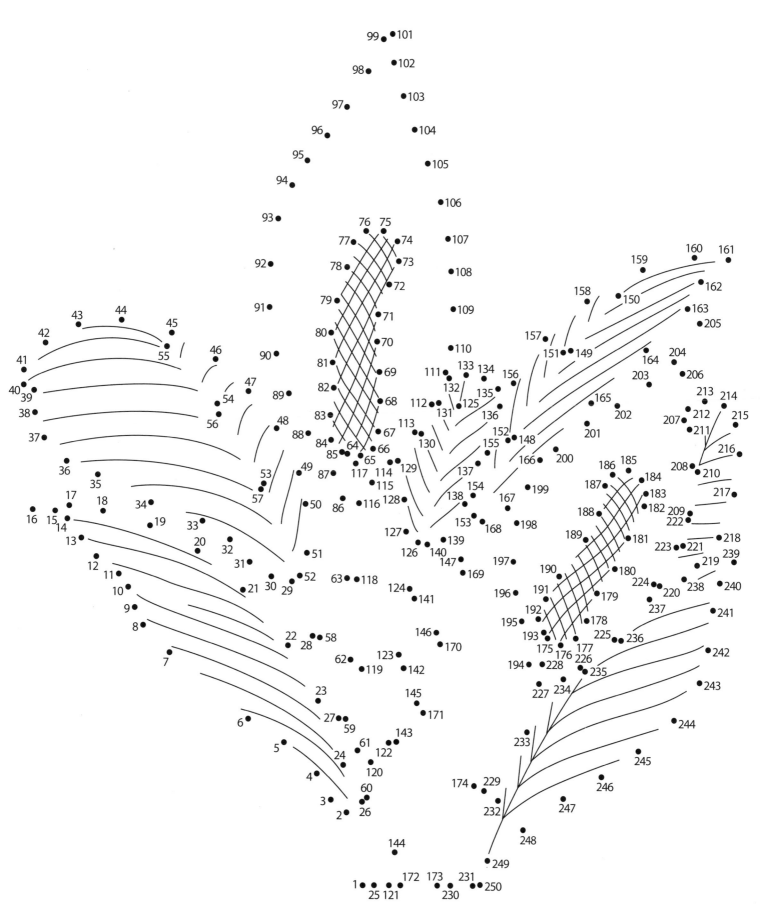

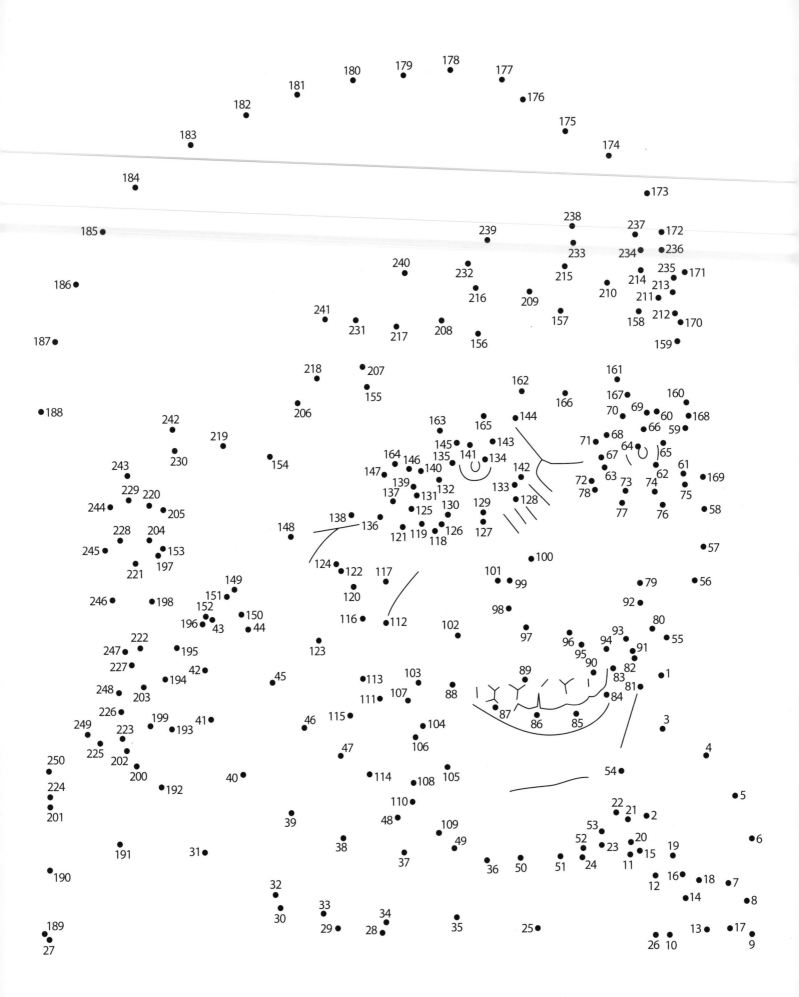

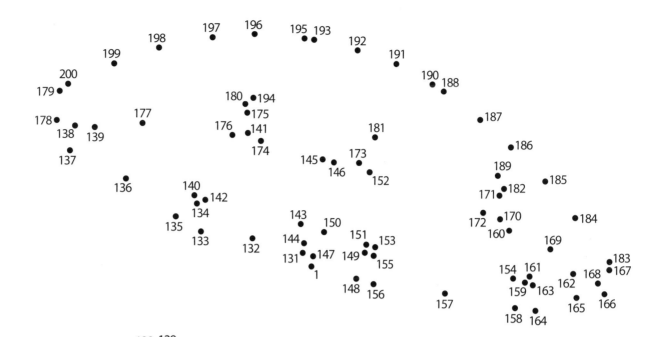
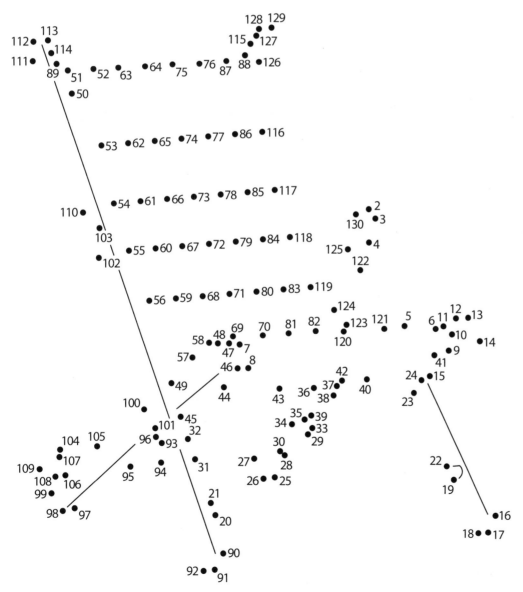

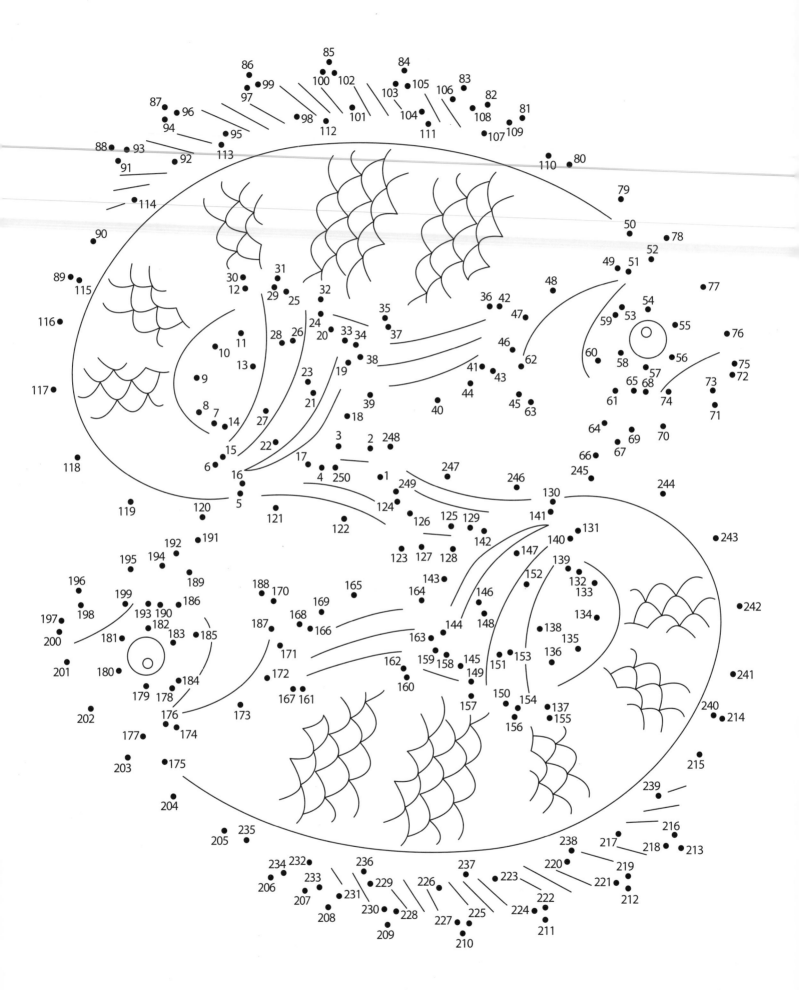

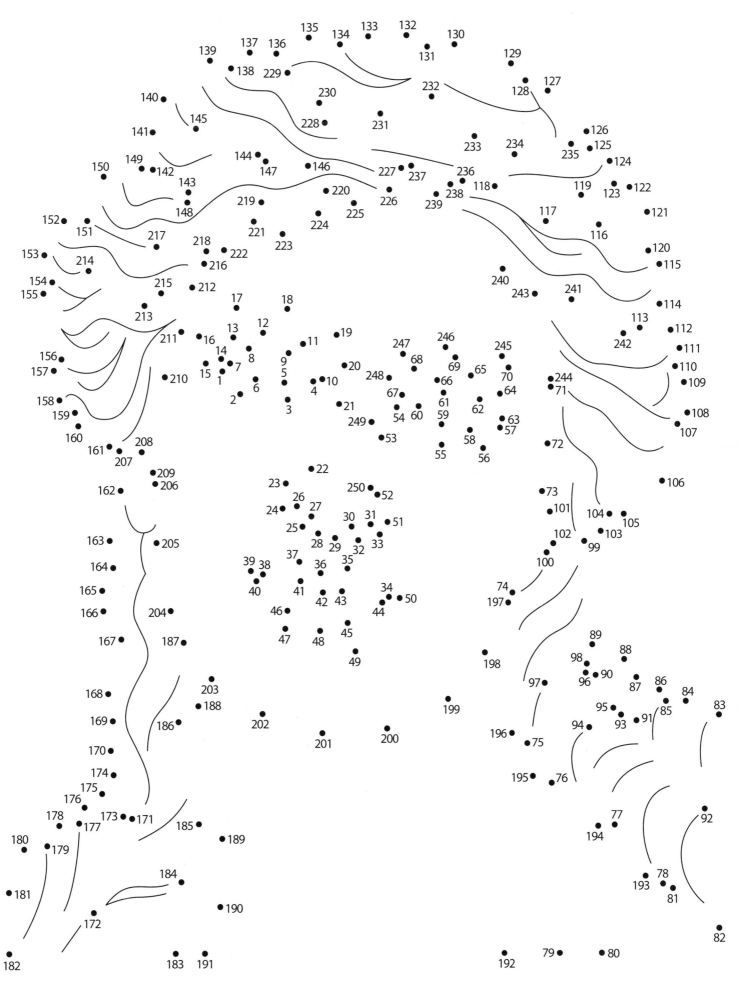

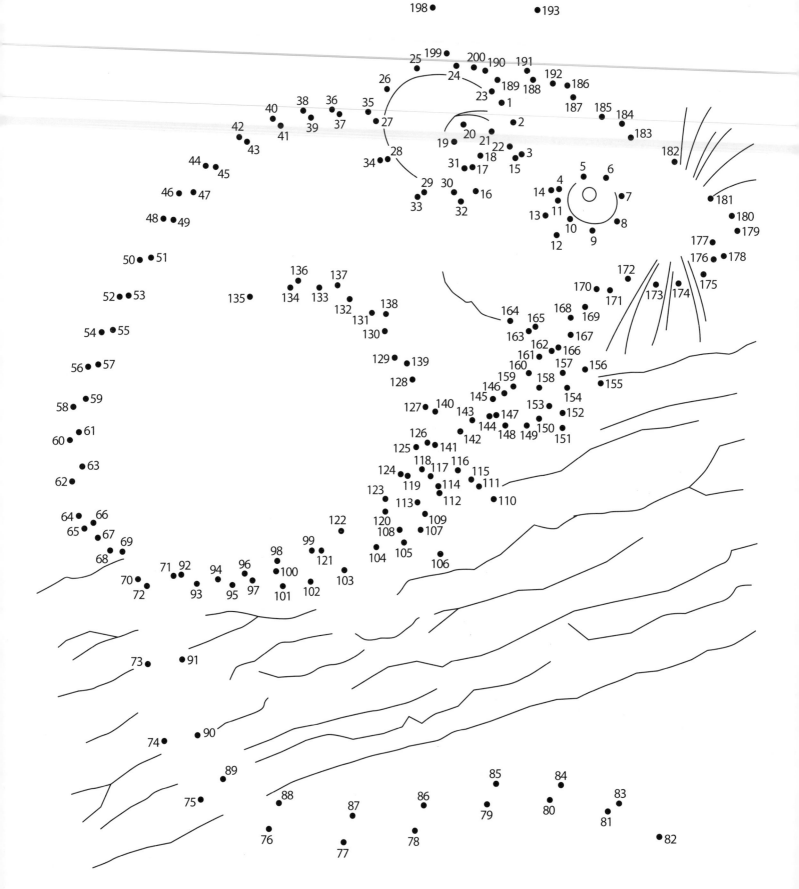

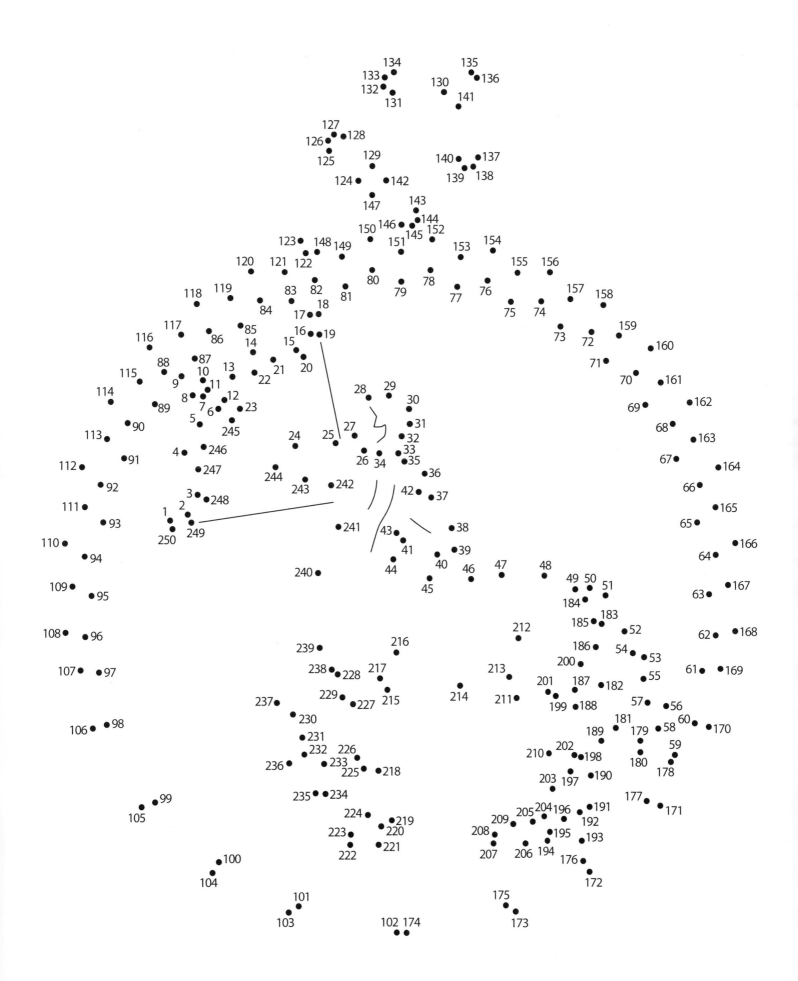

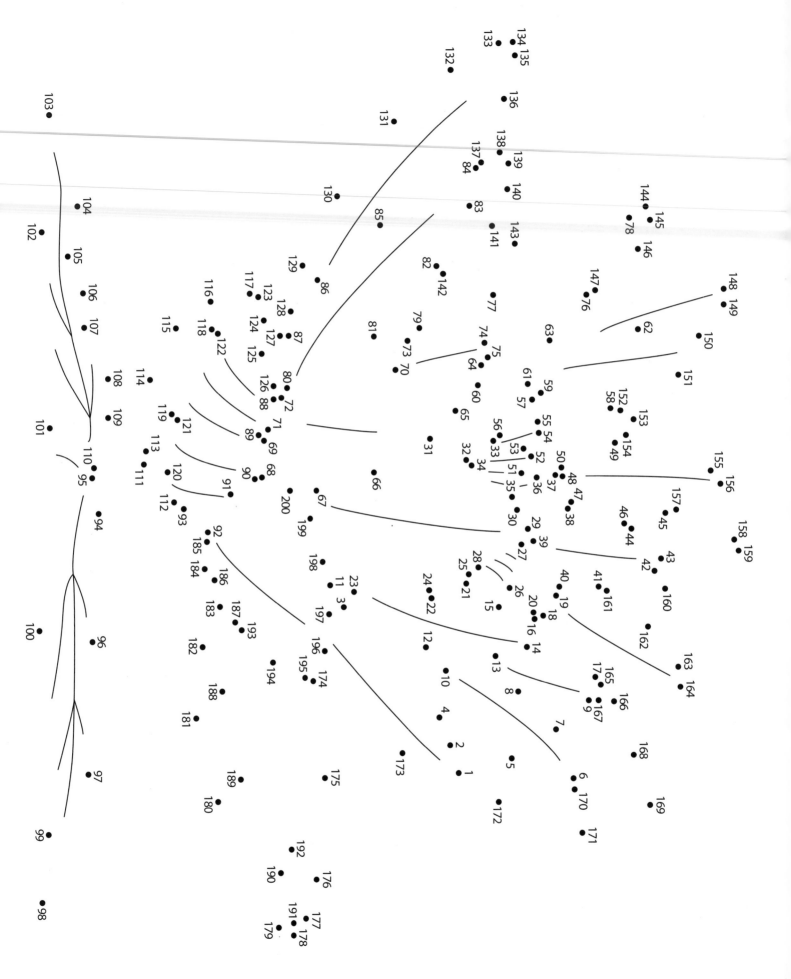

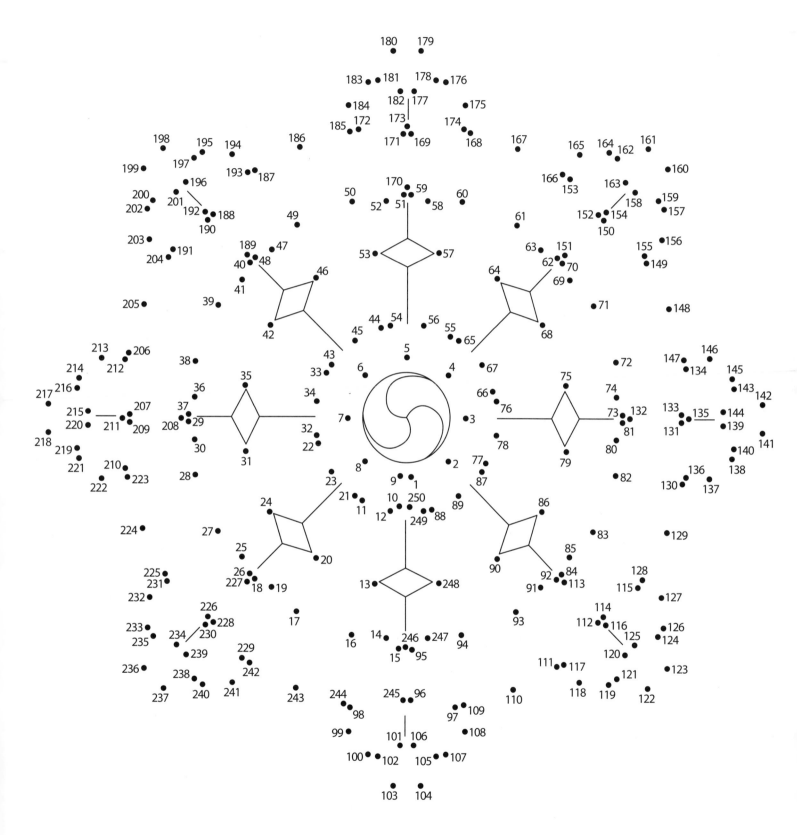

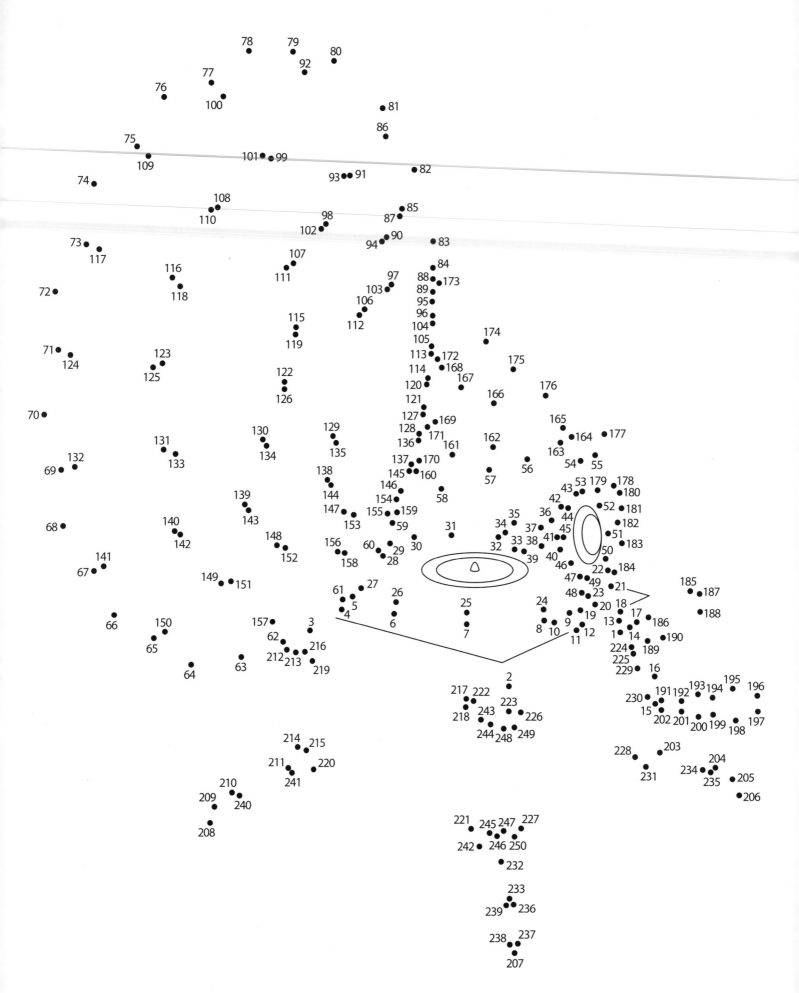

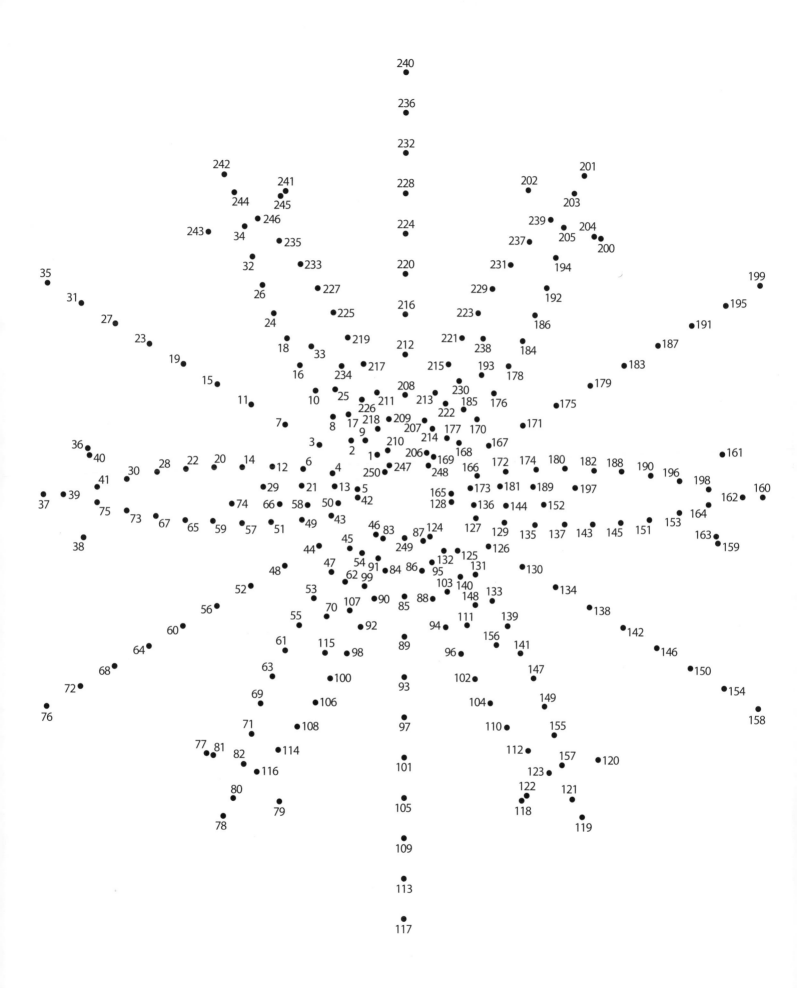

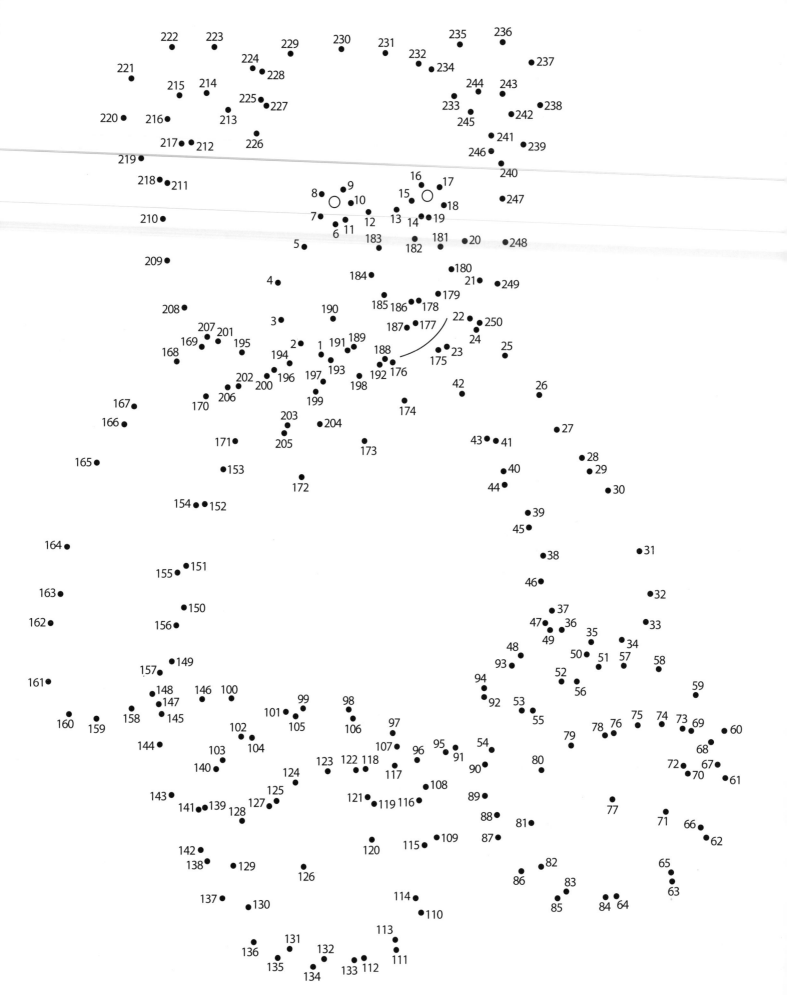

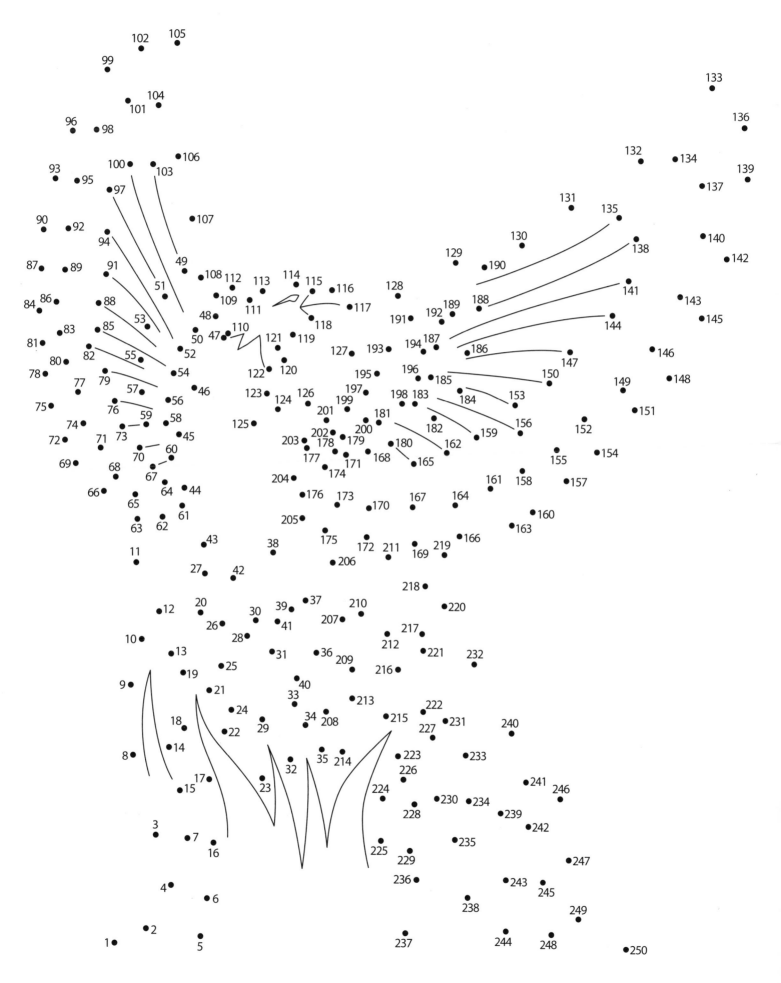

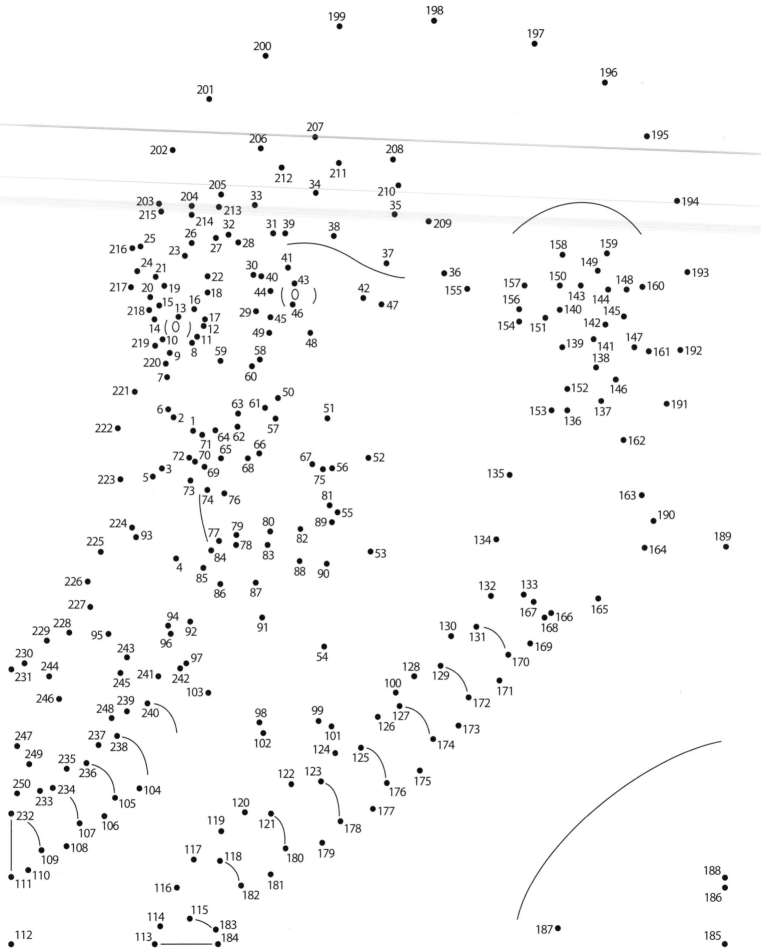

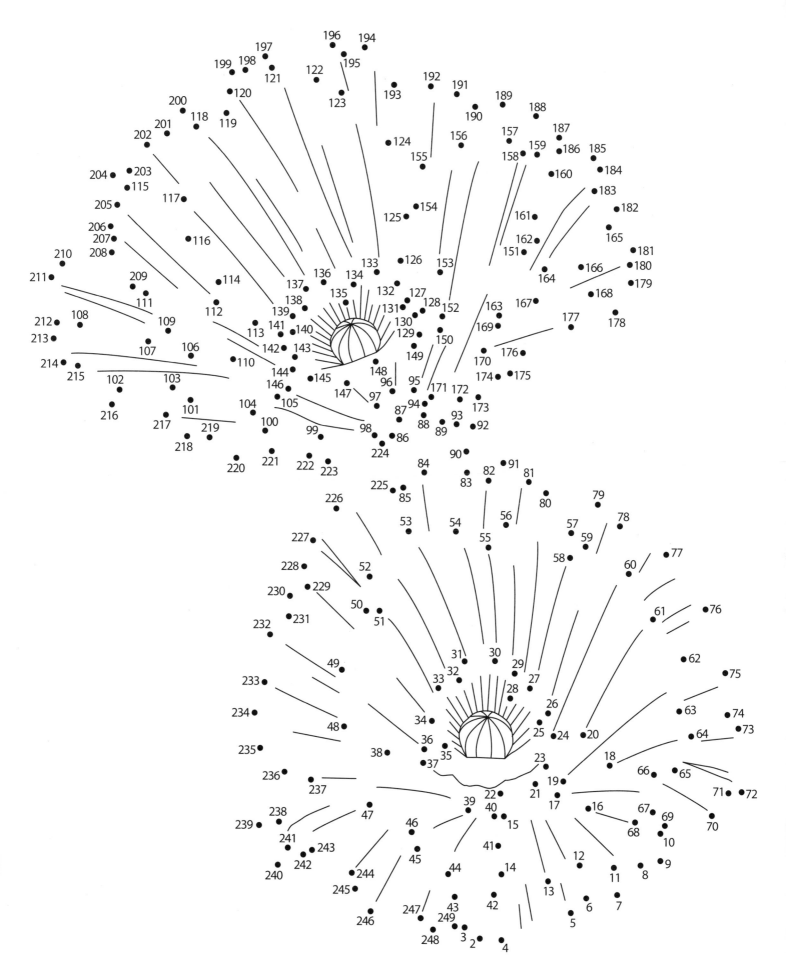

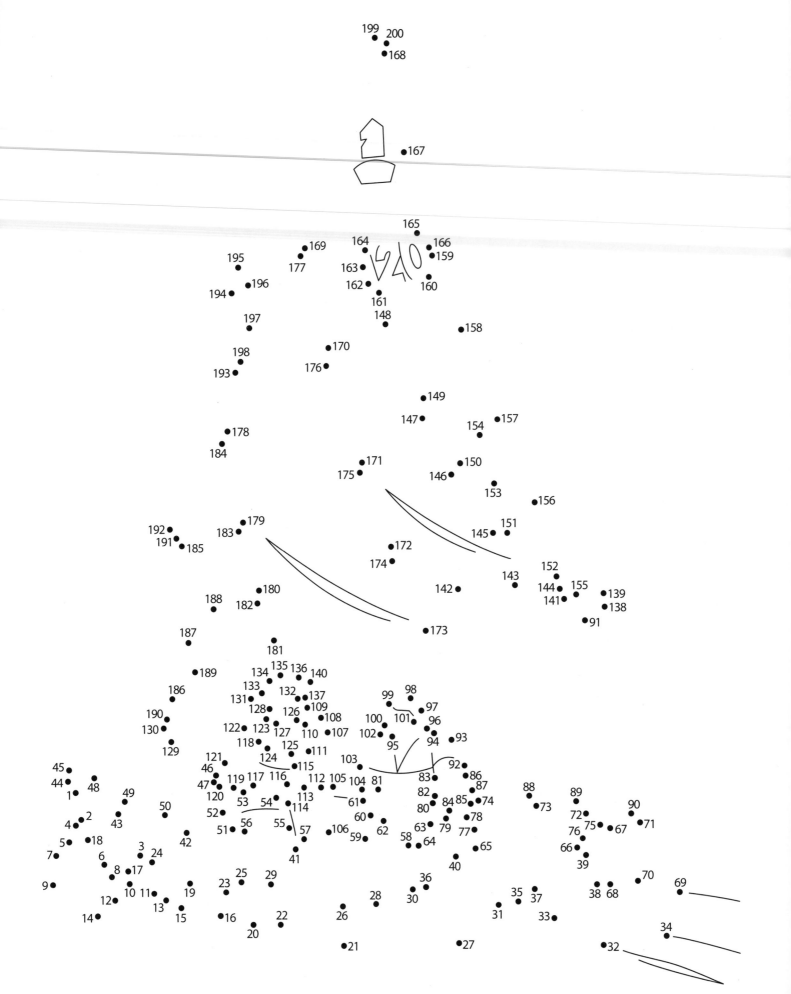

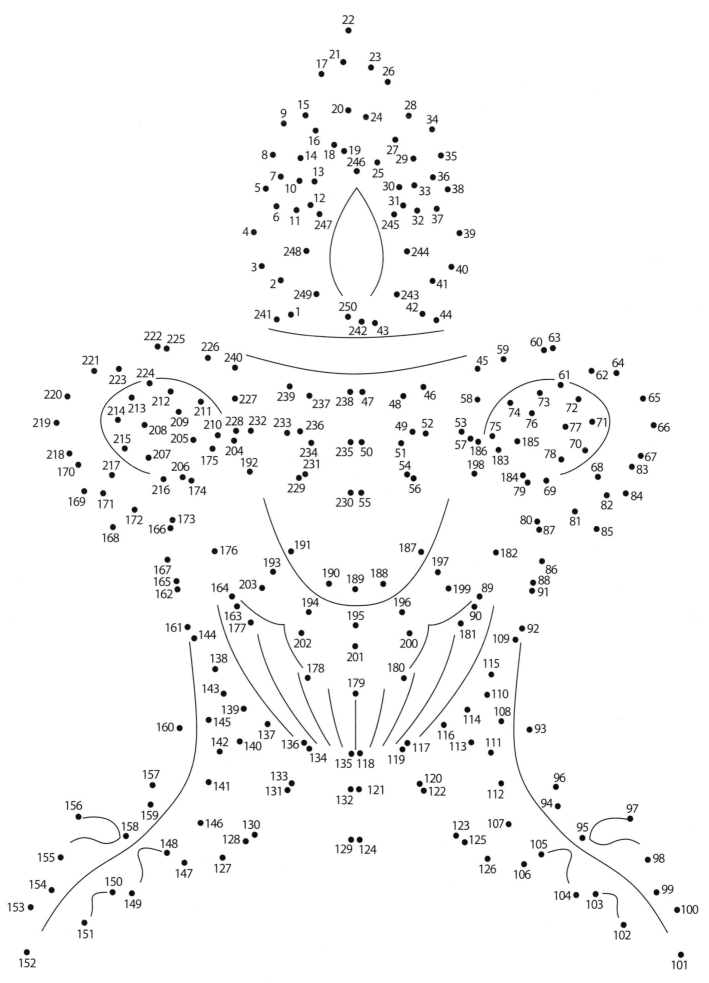

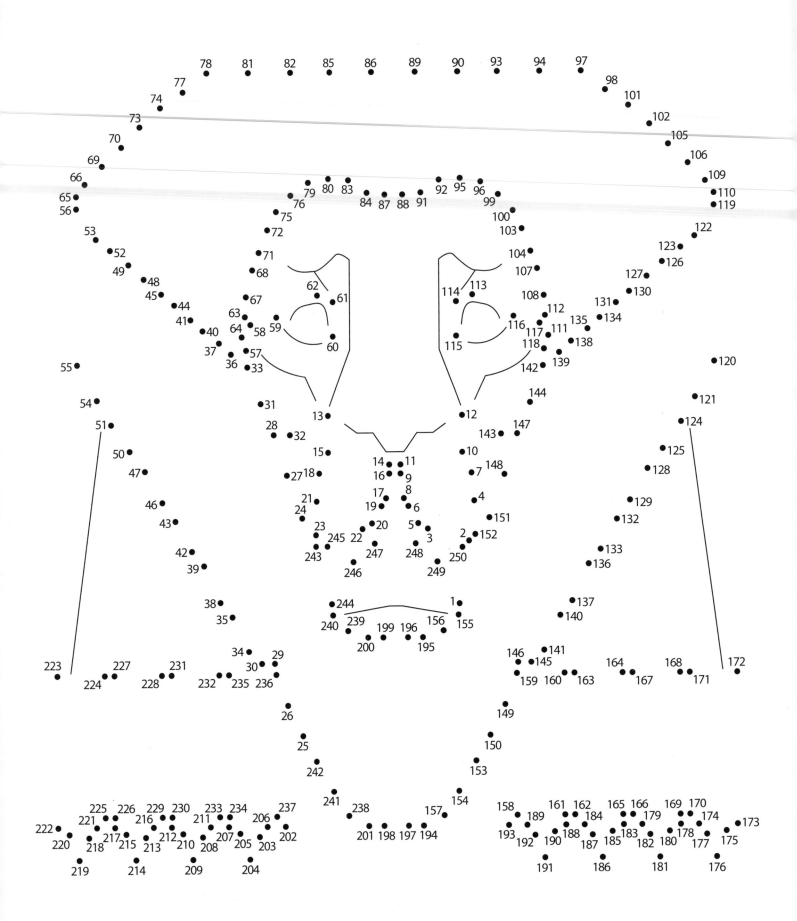

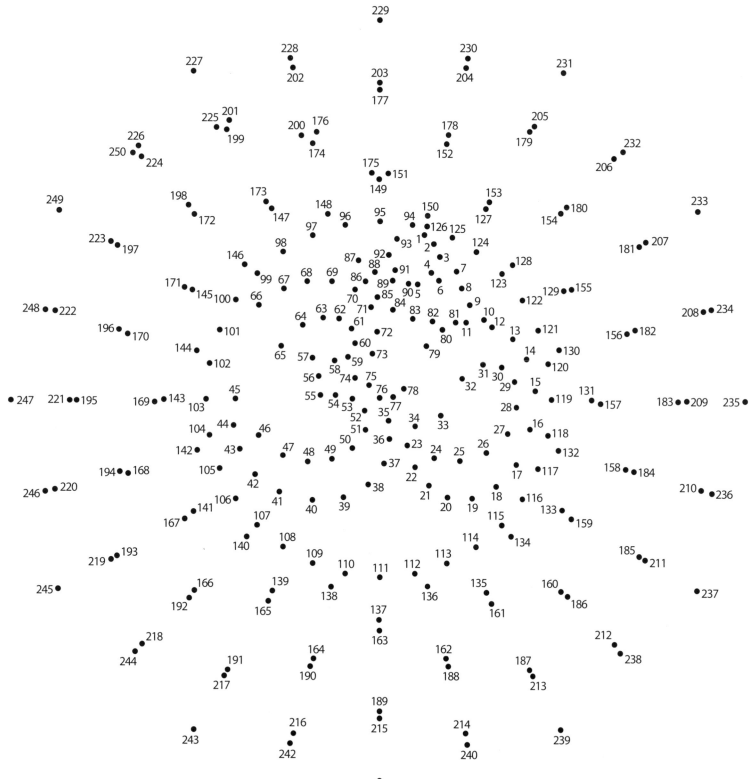

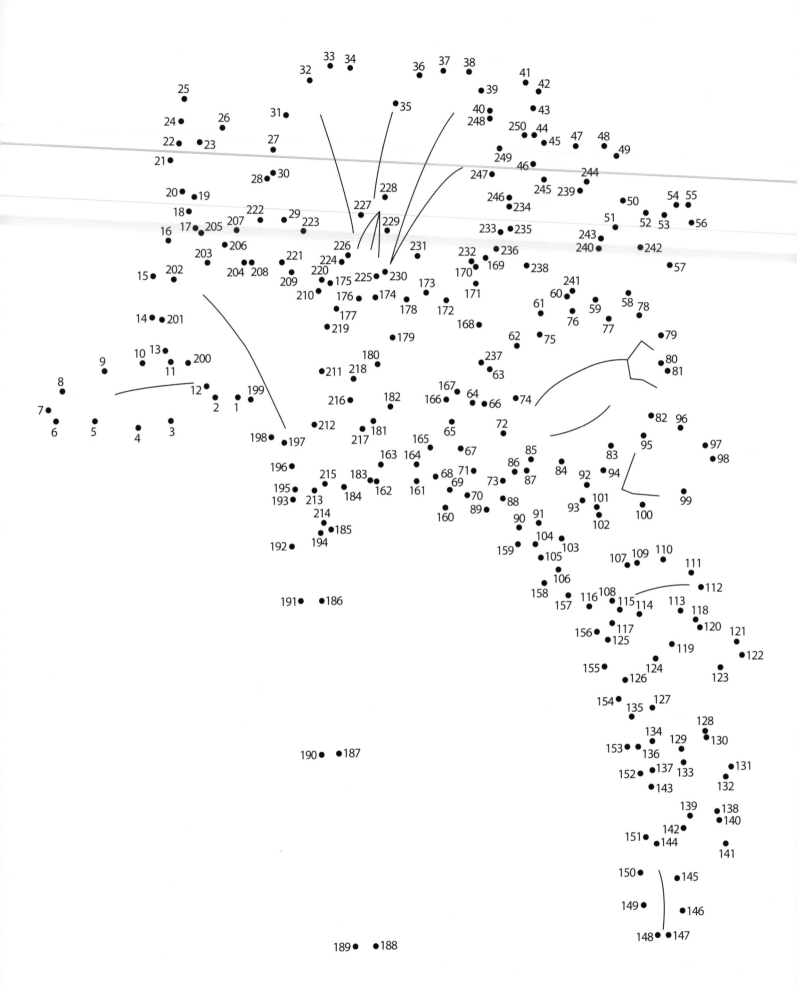

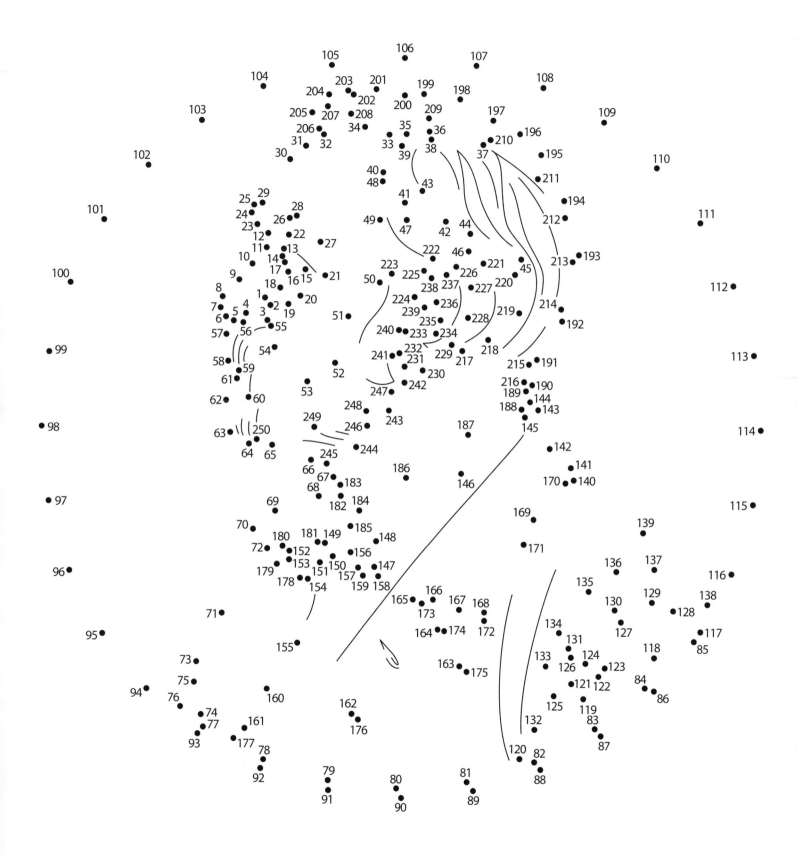

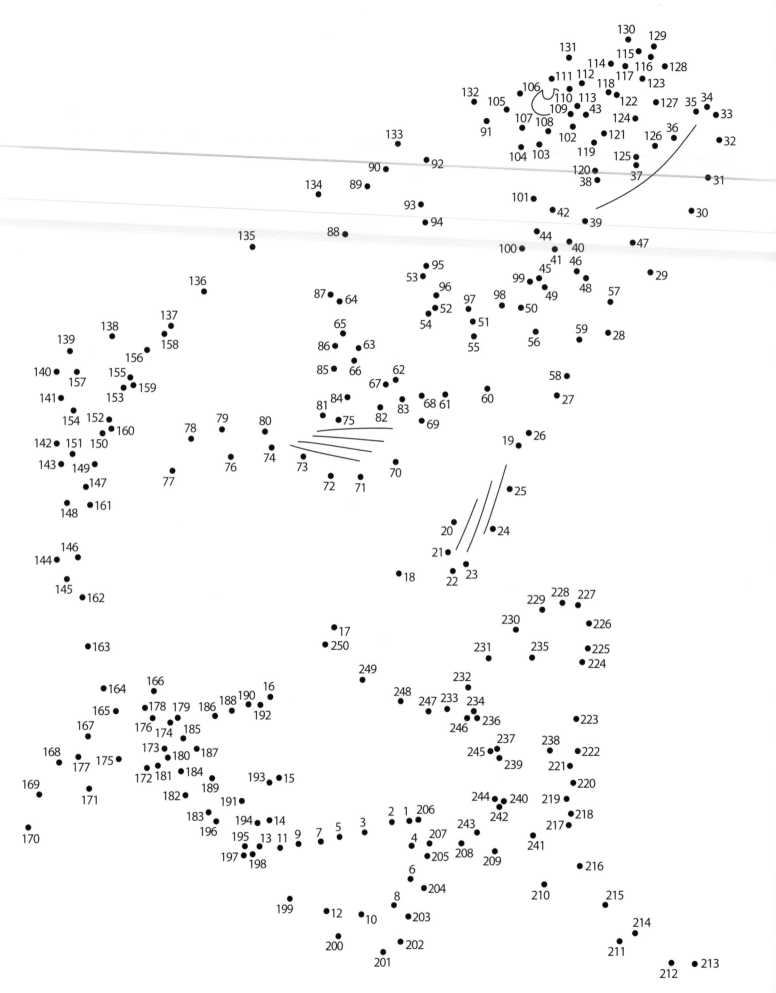

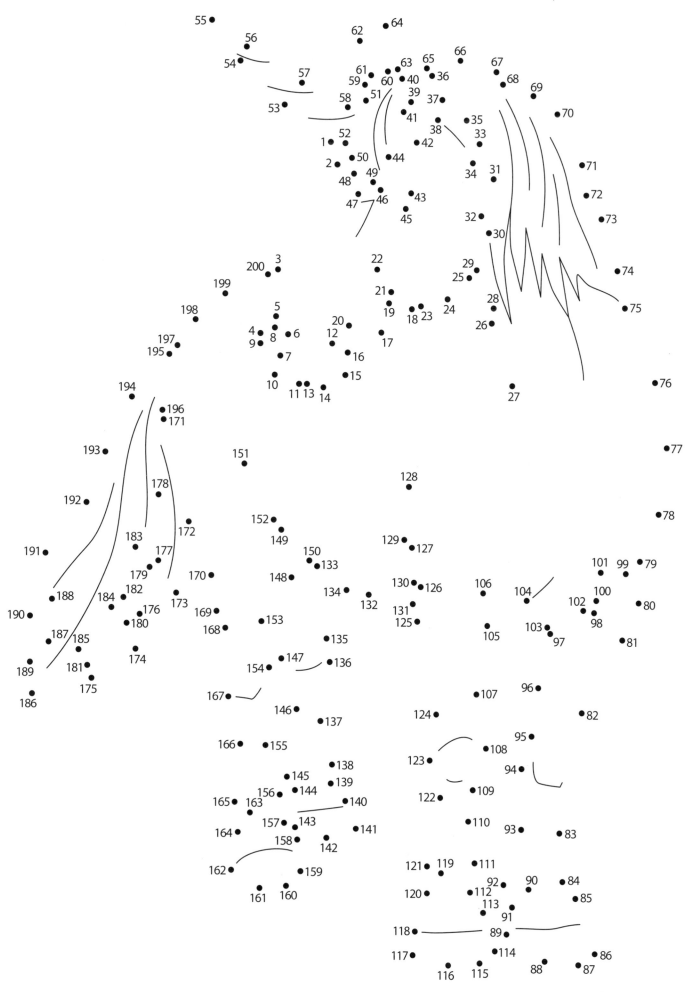

85

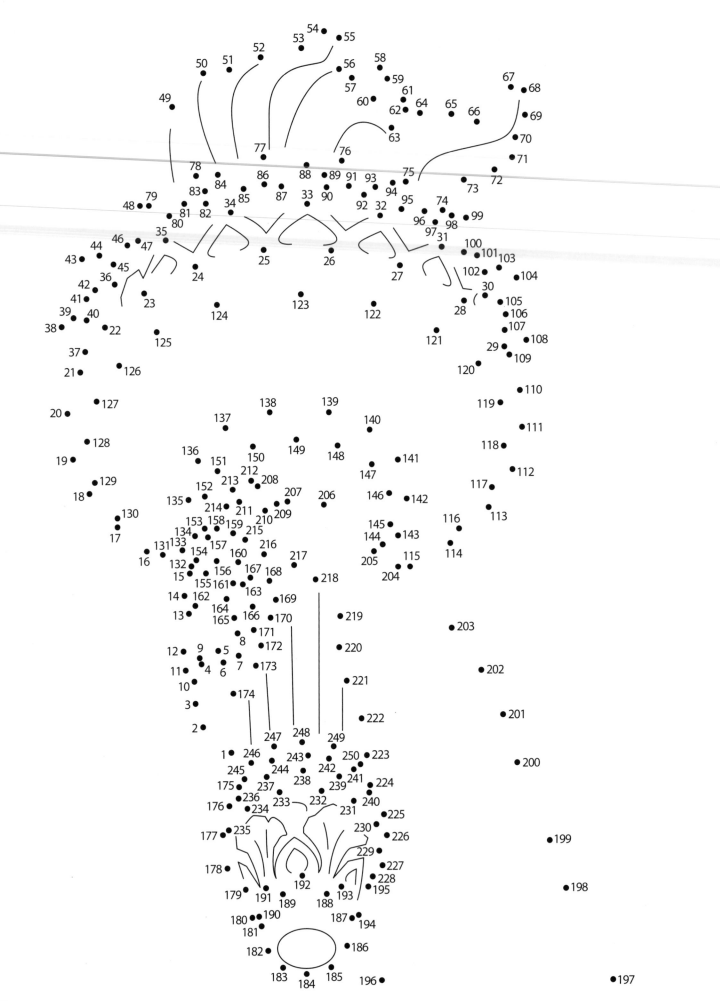

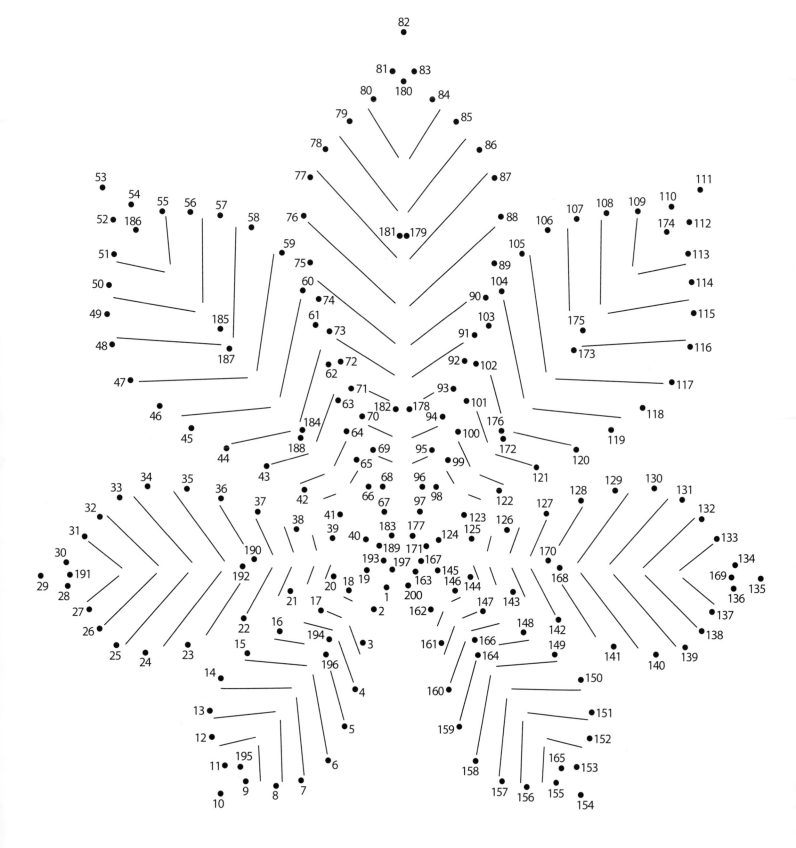

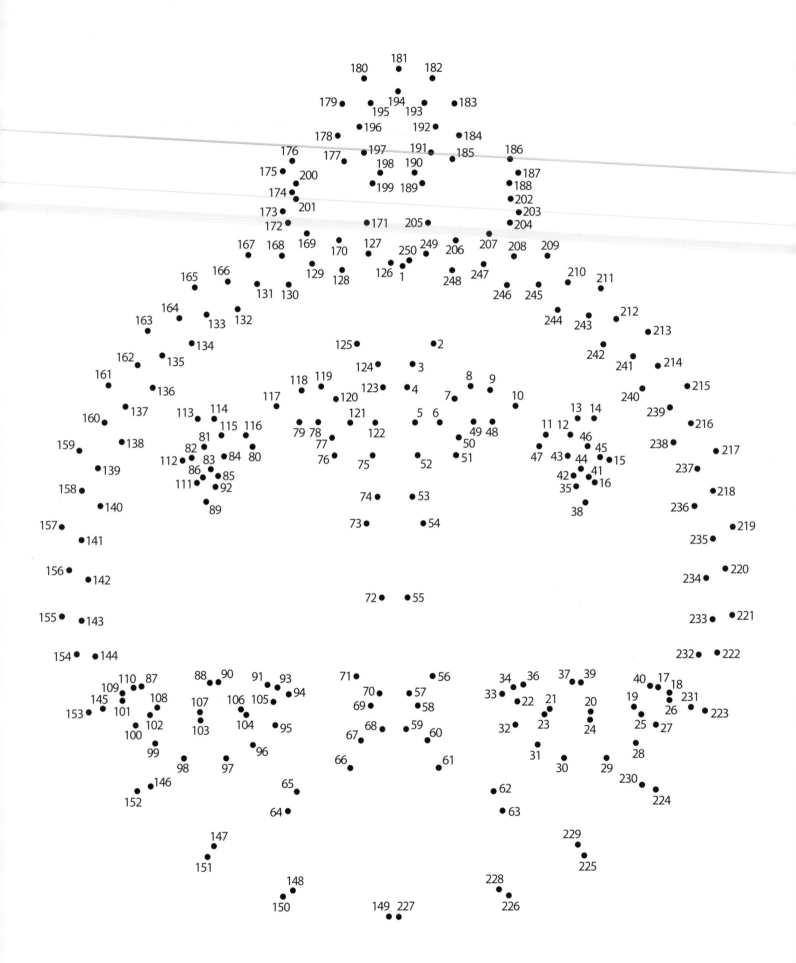

89

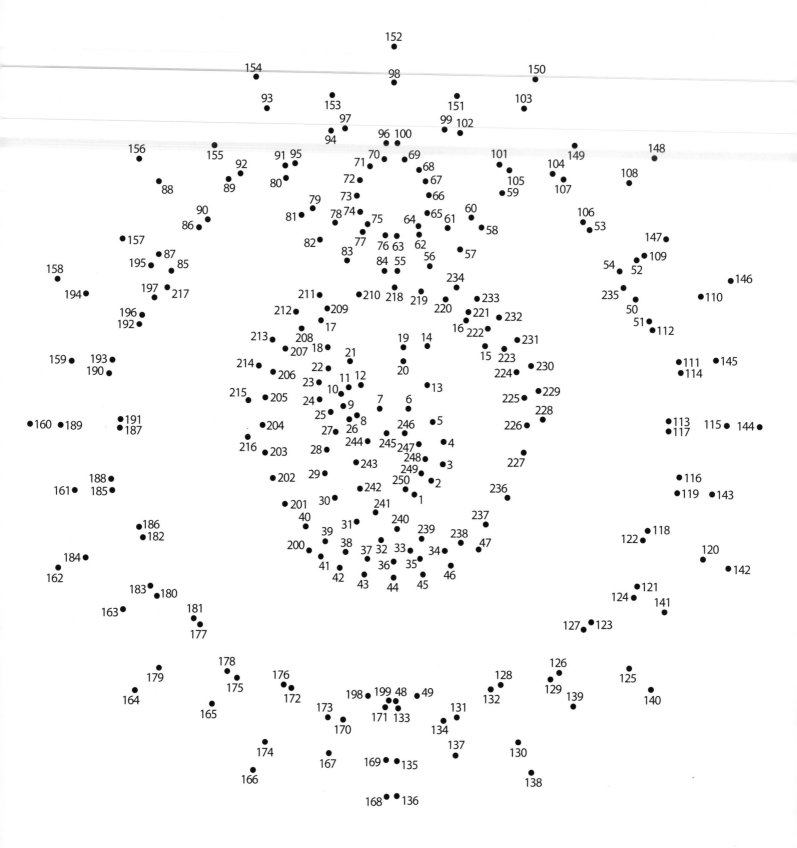

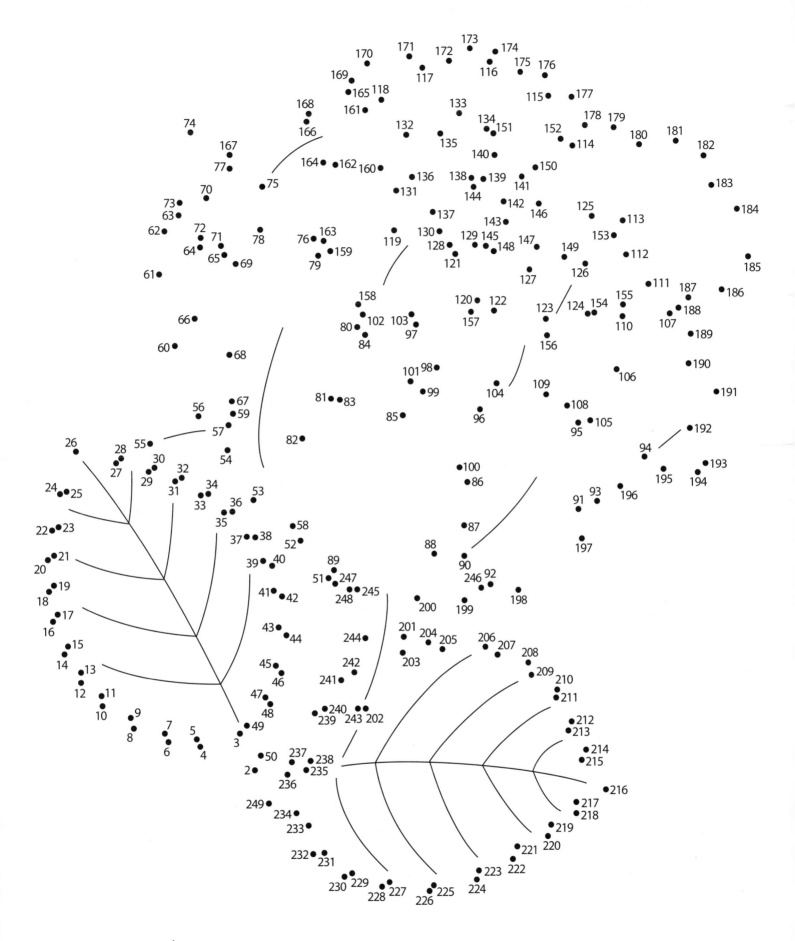

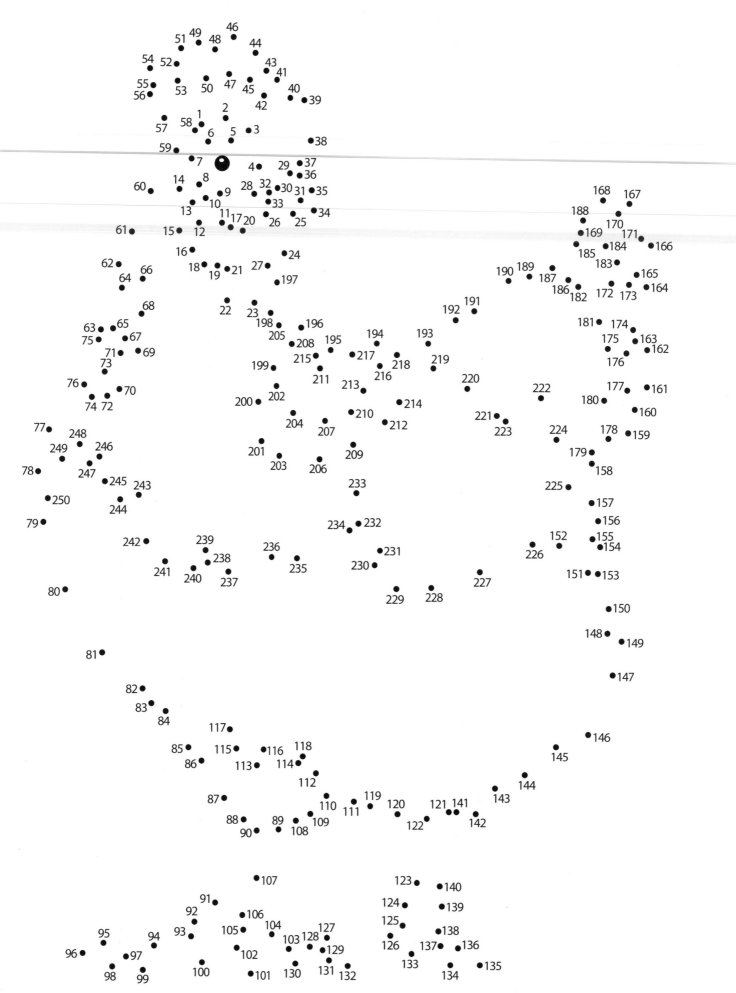

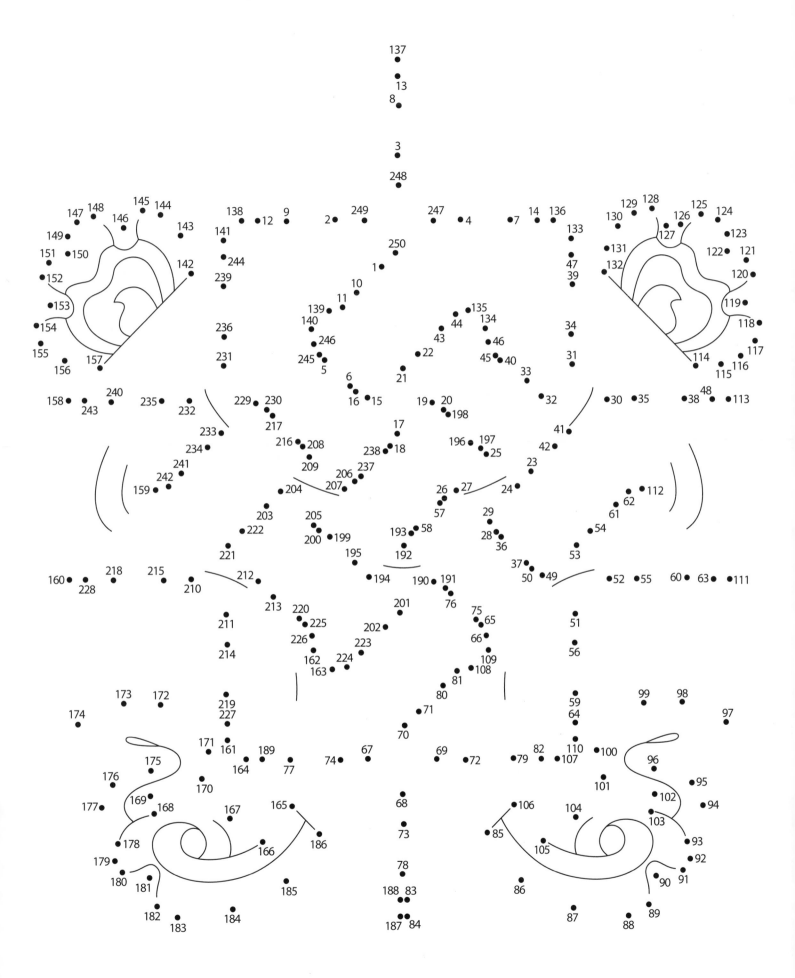

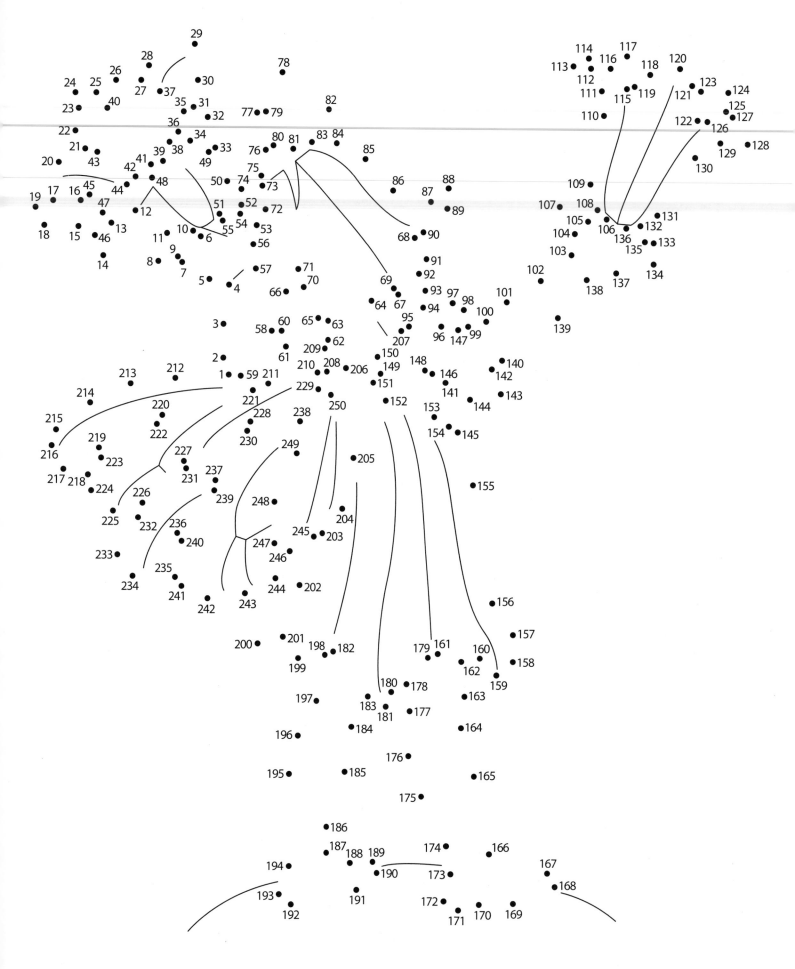

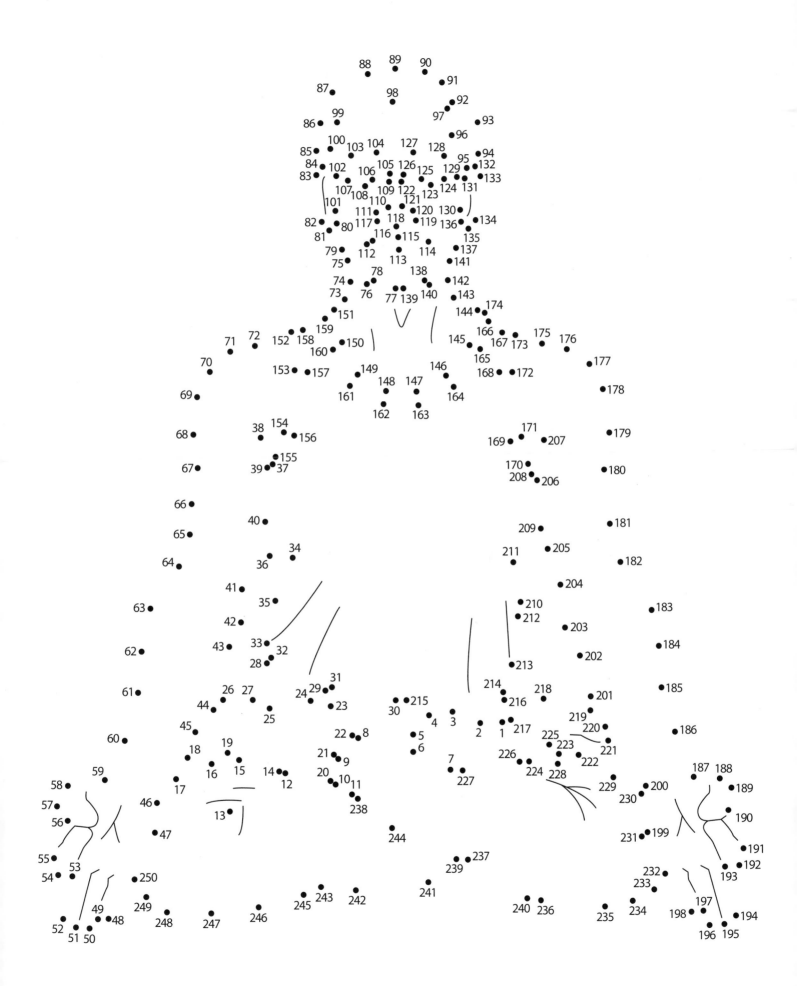

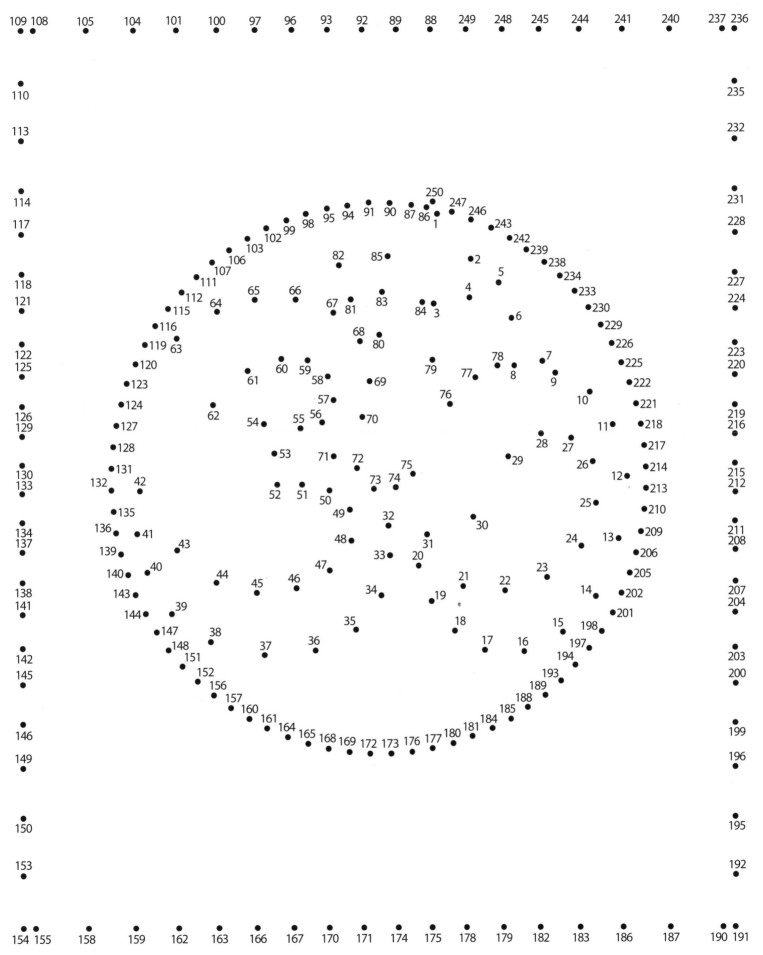

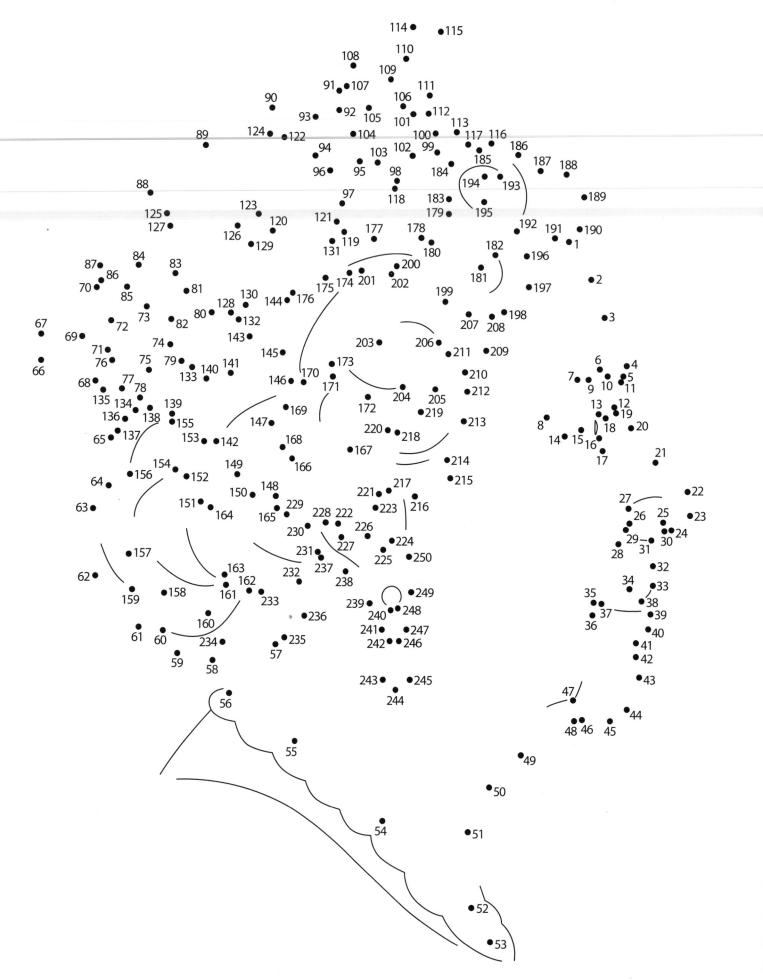

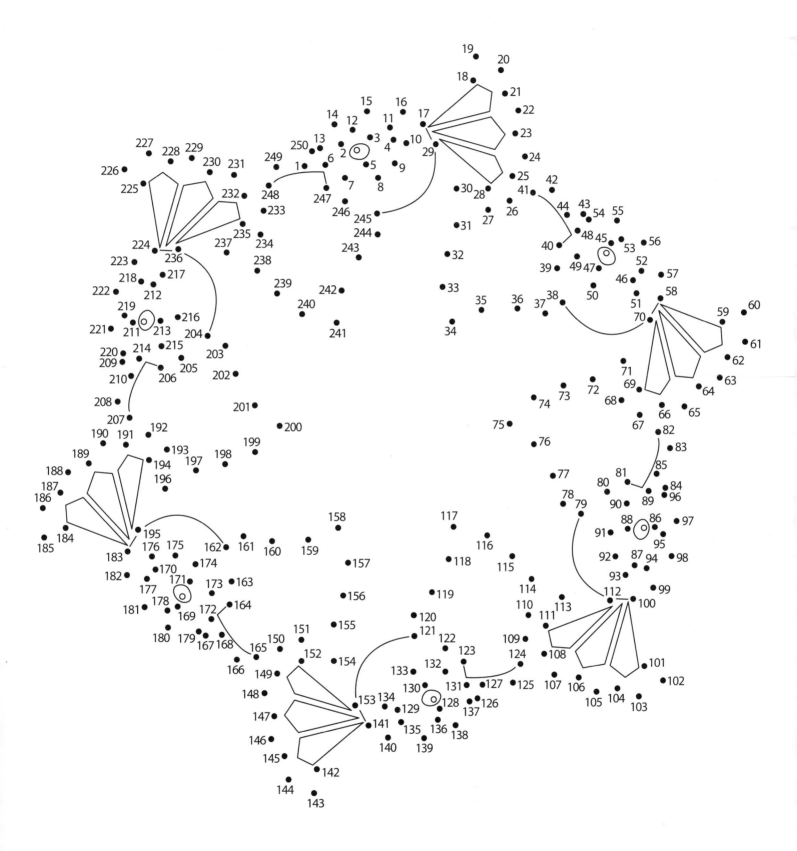

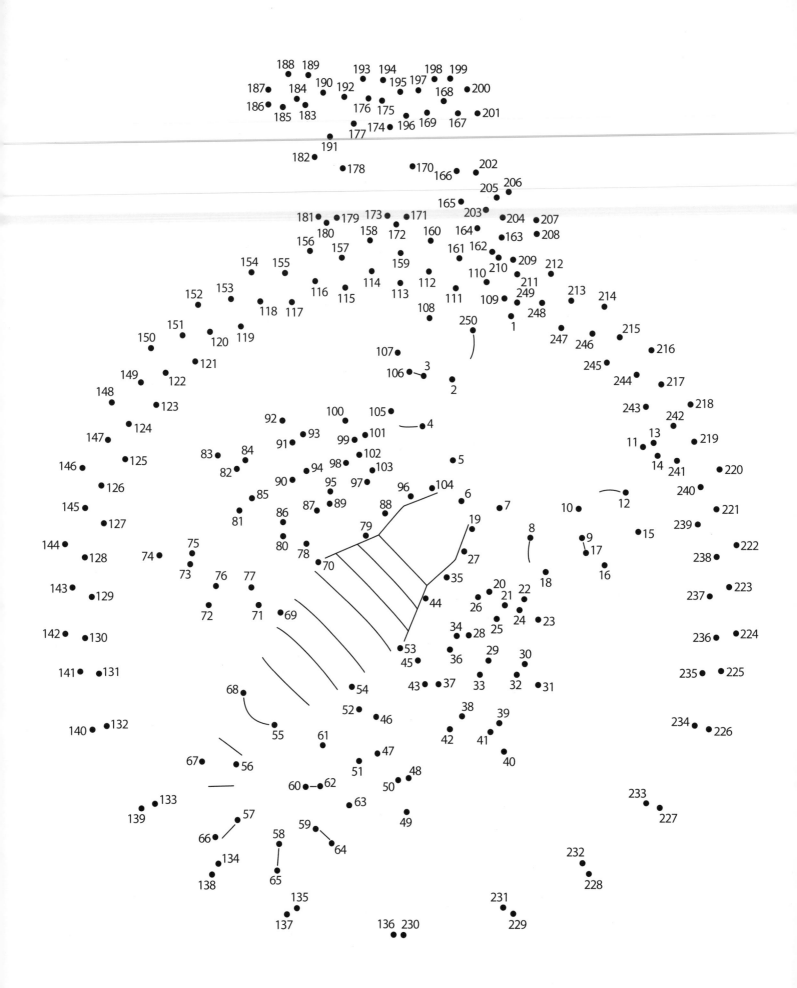

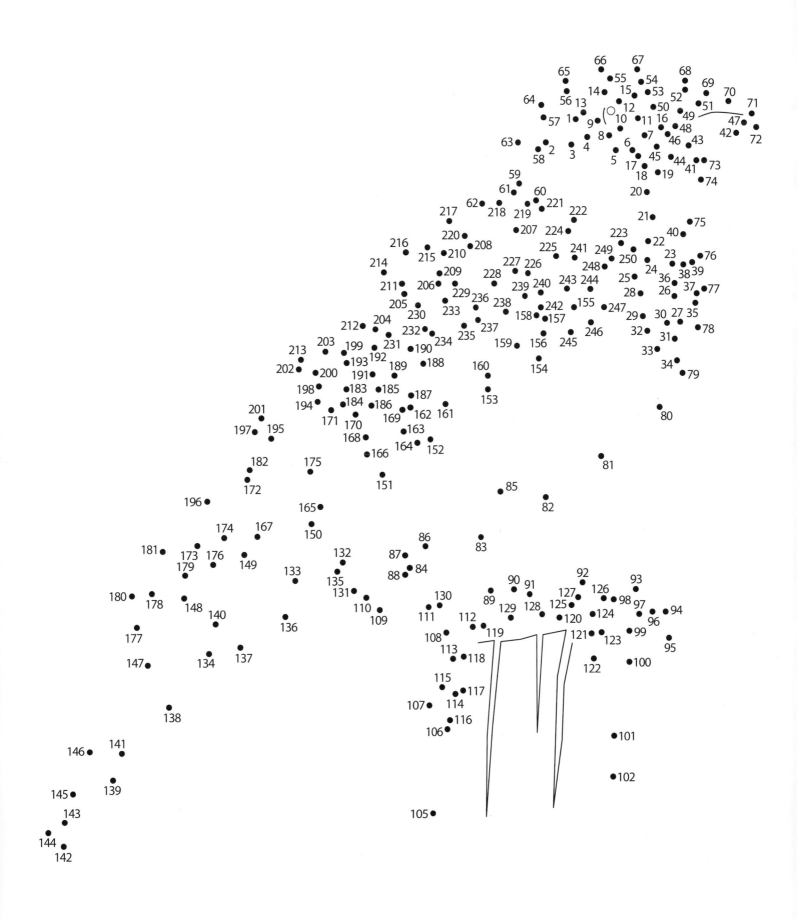

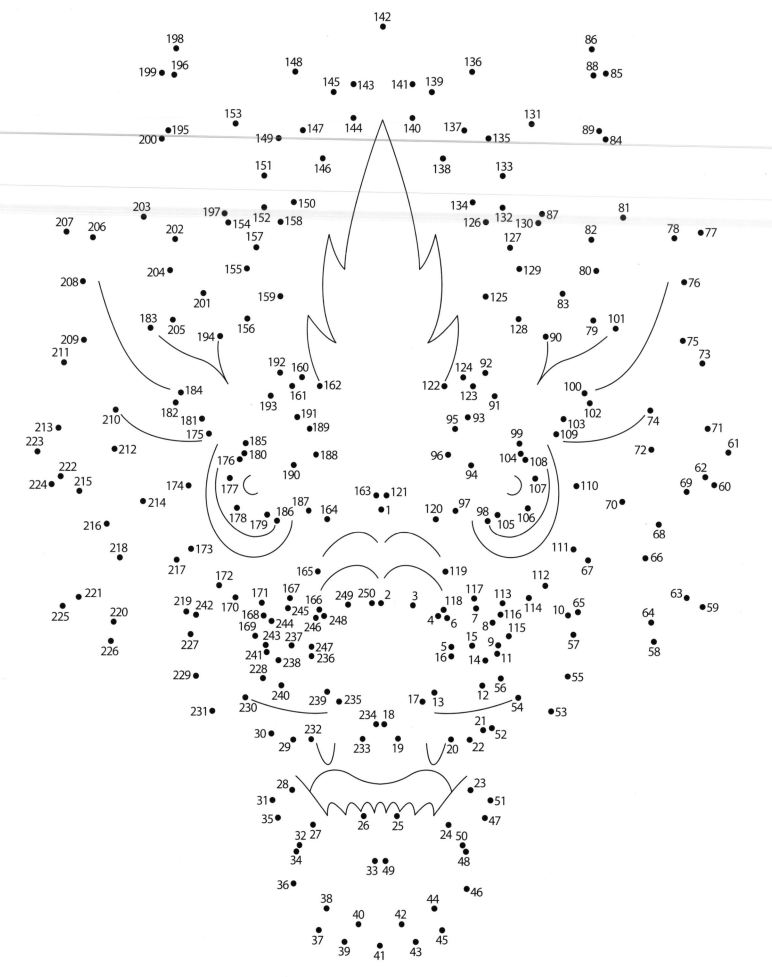

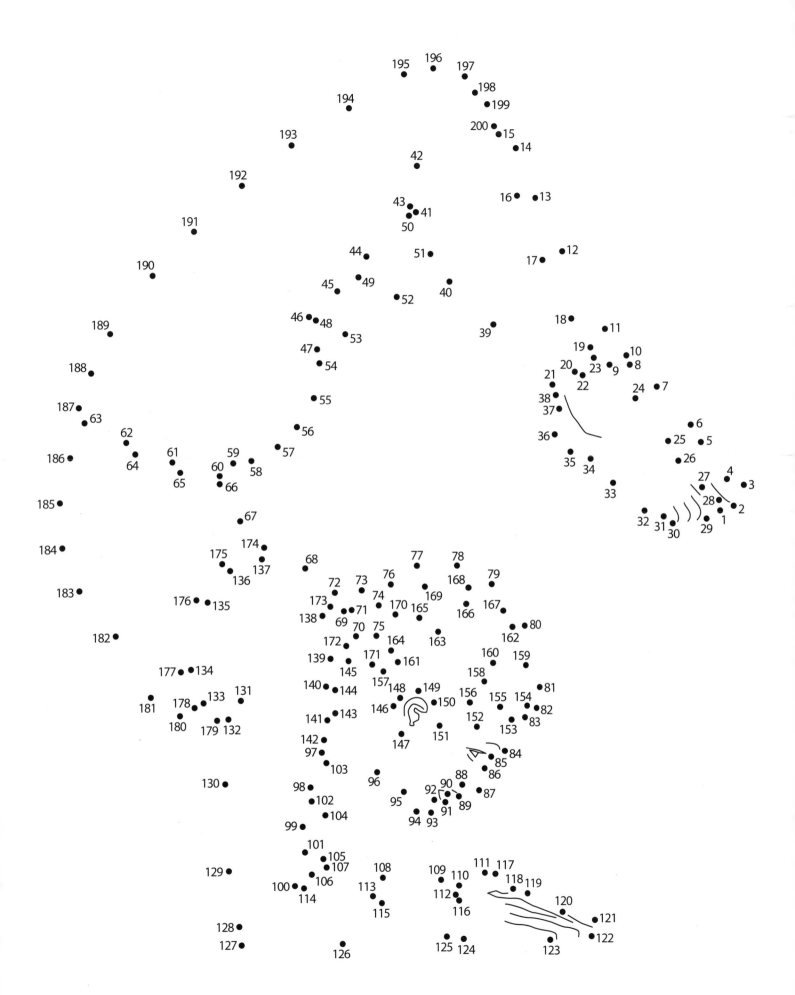

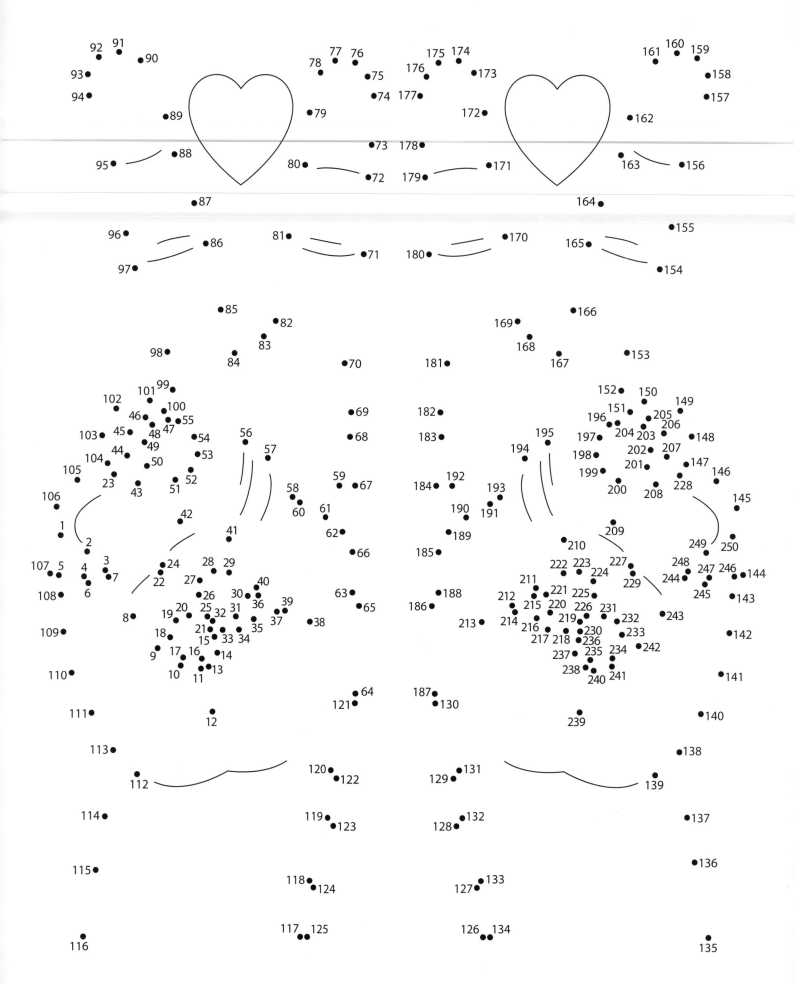

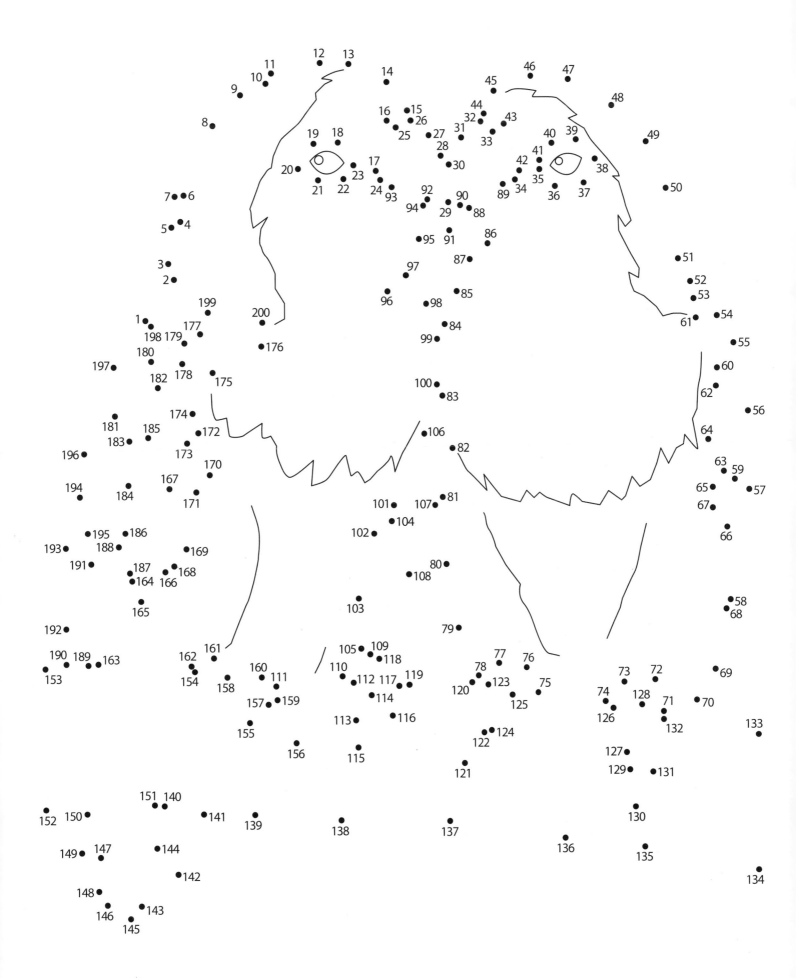

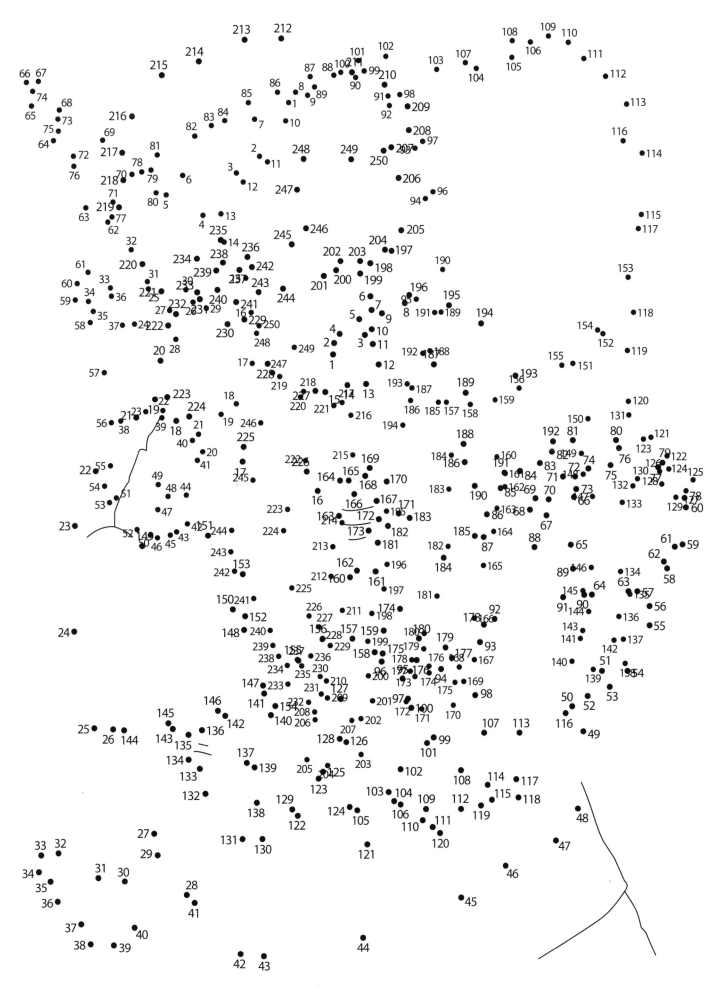

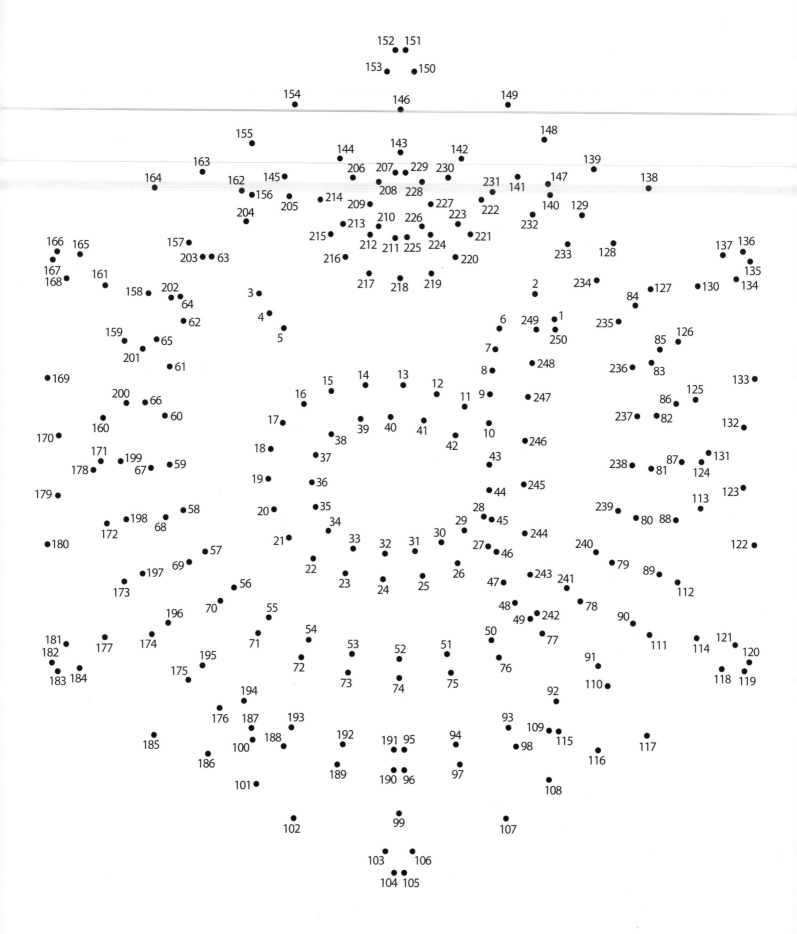

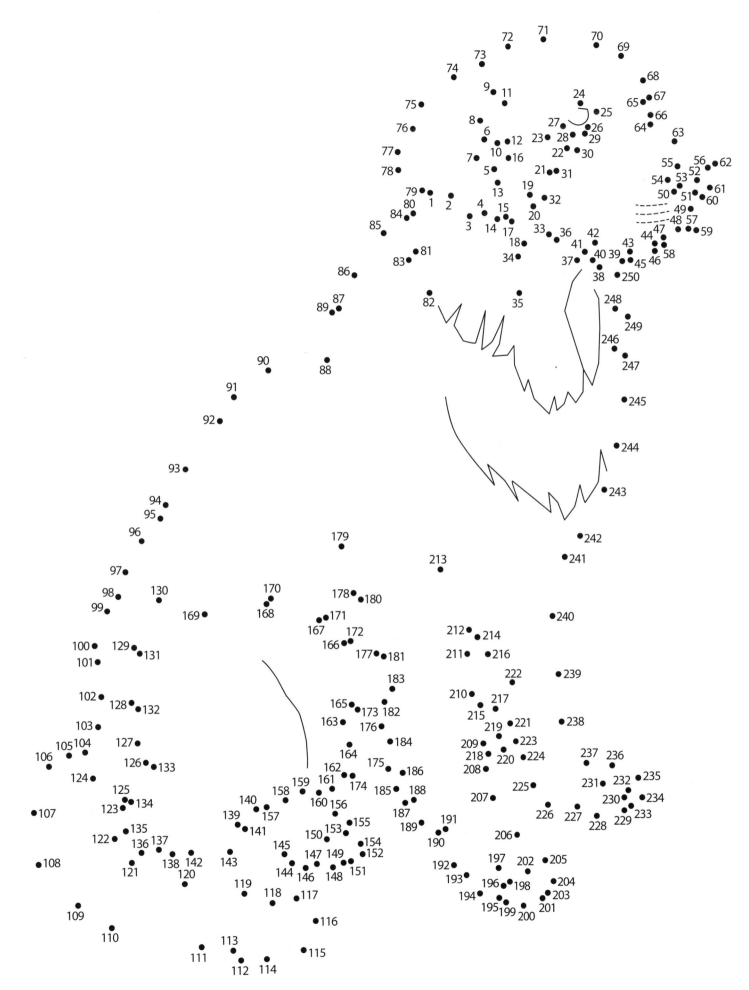

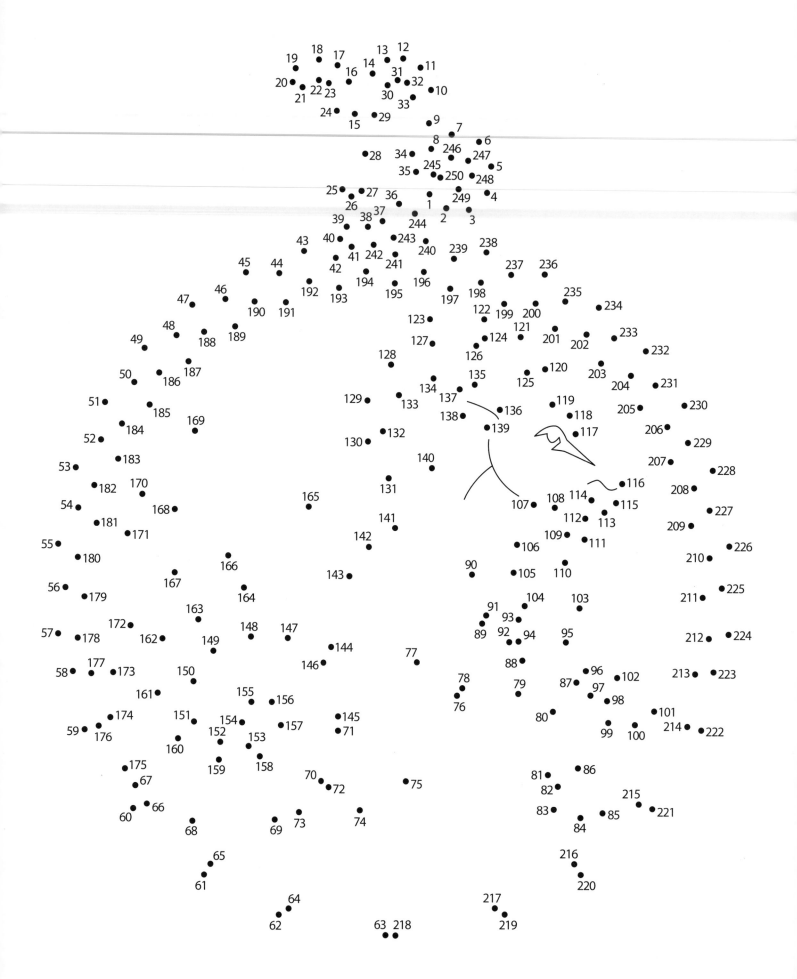

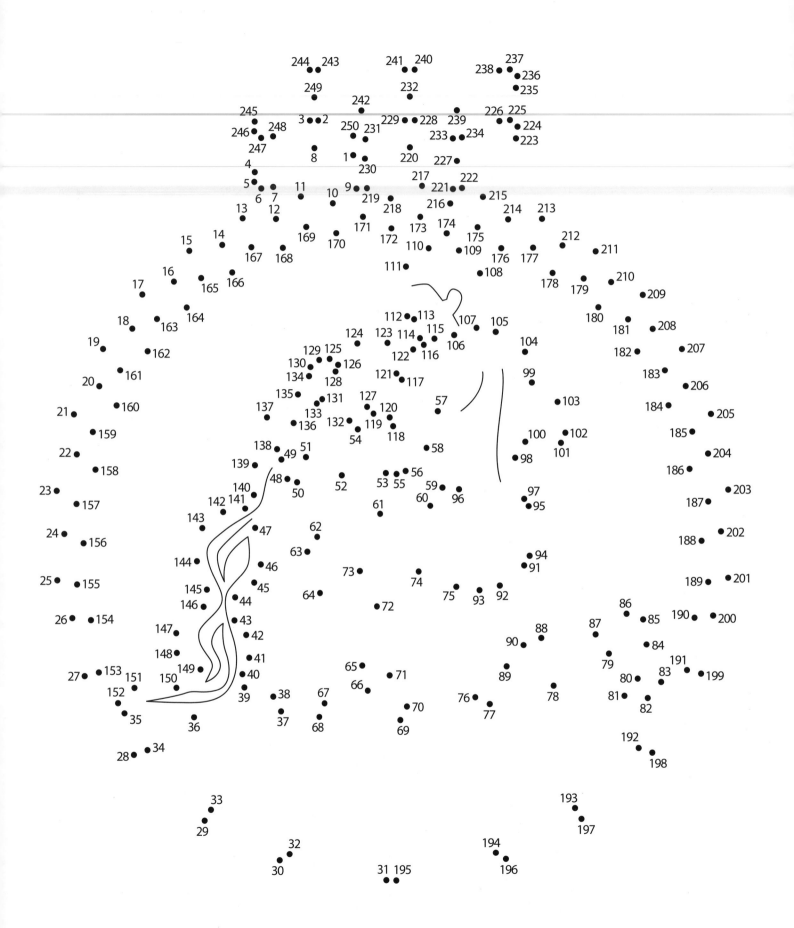

112

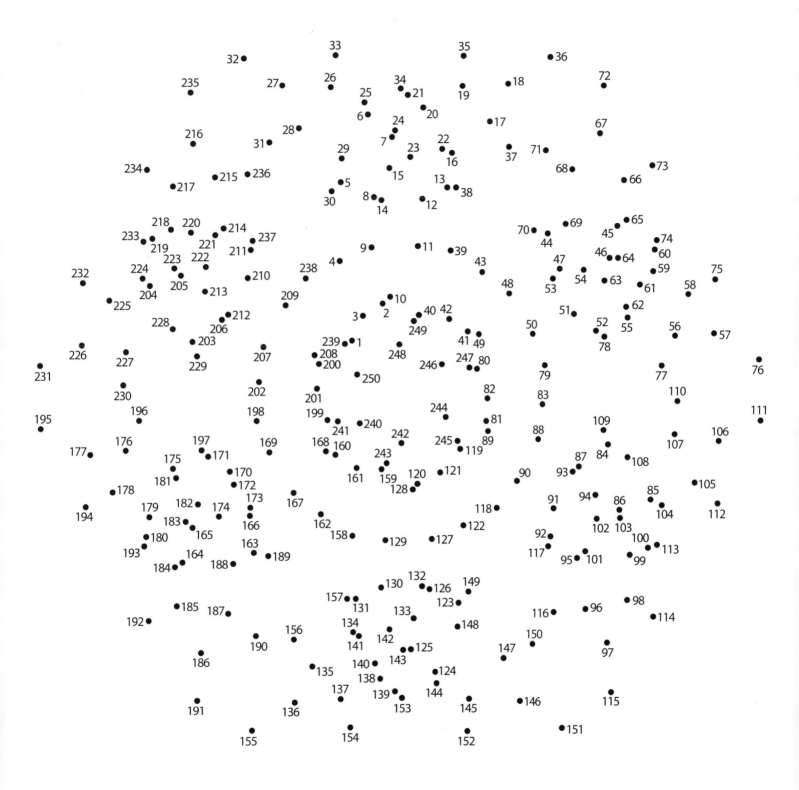

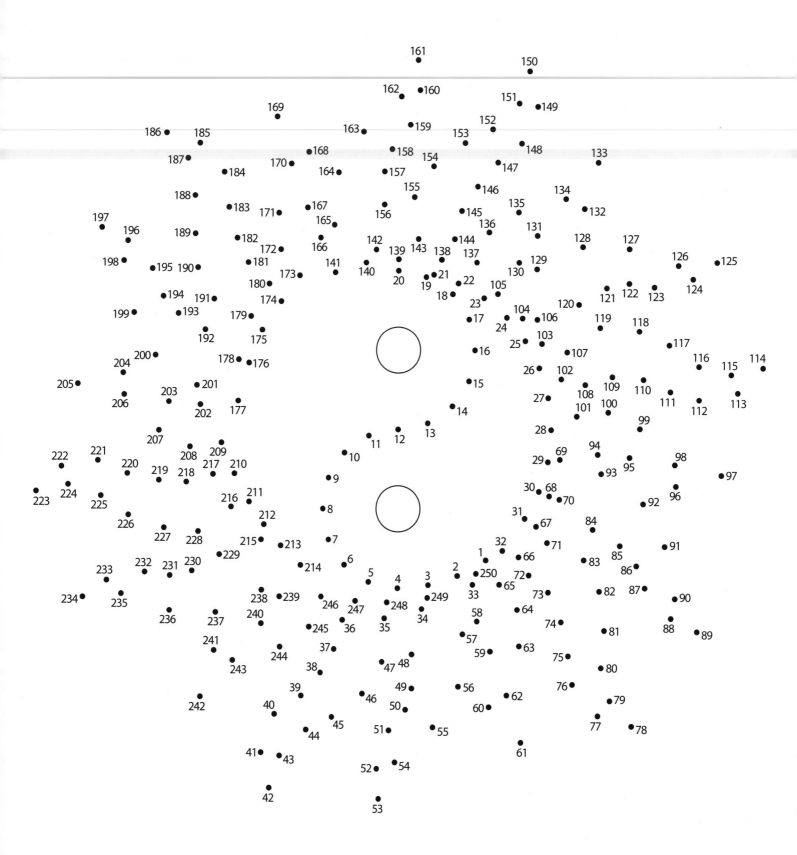

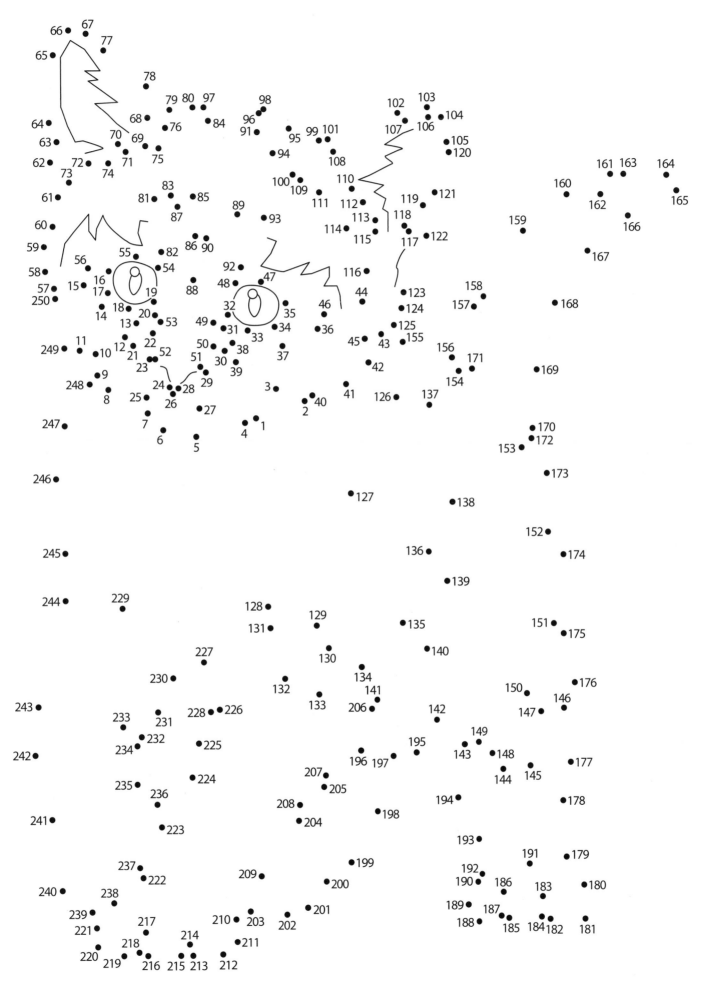

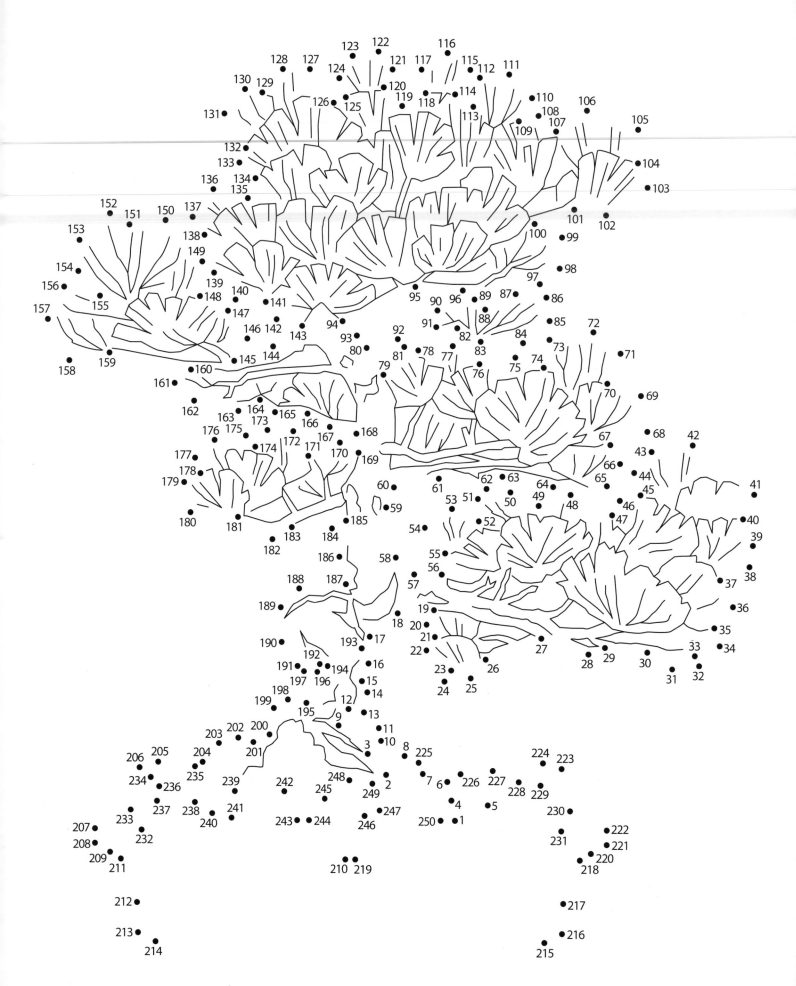

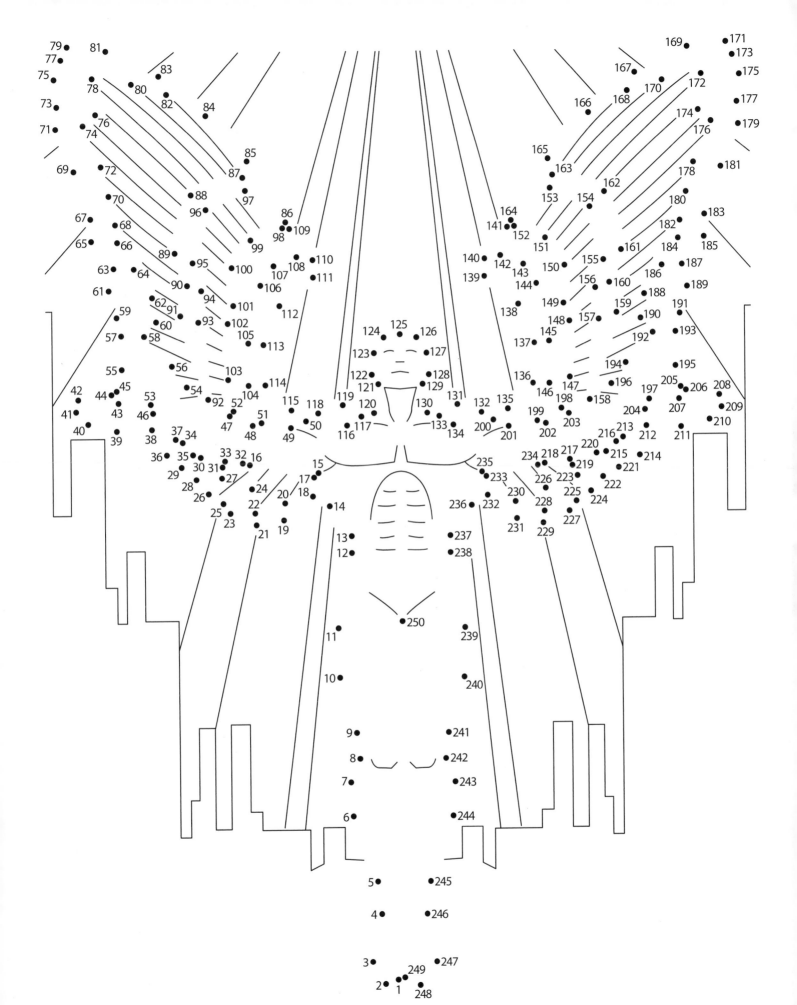

117

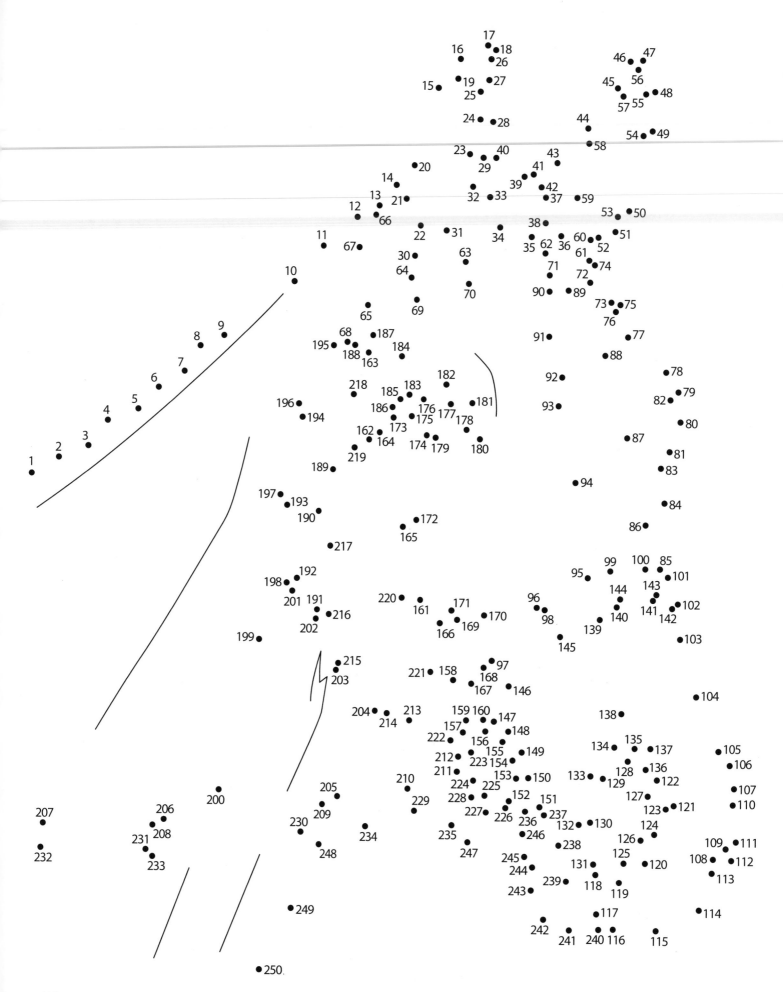

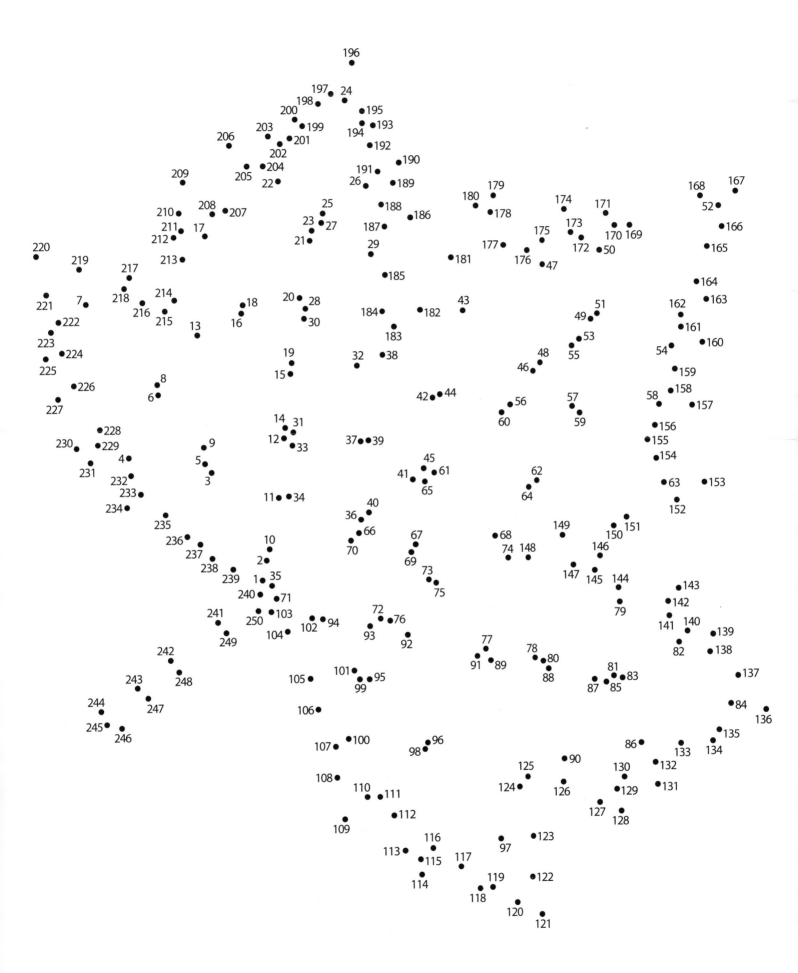

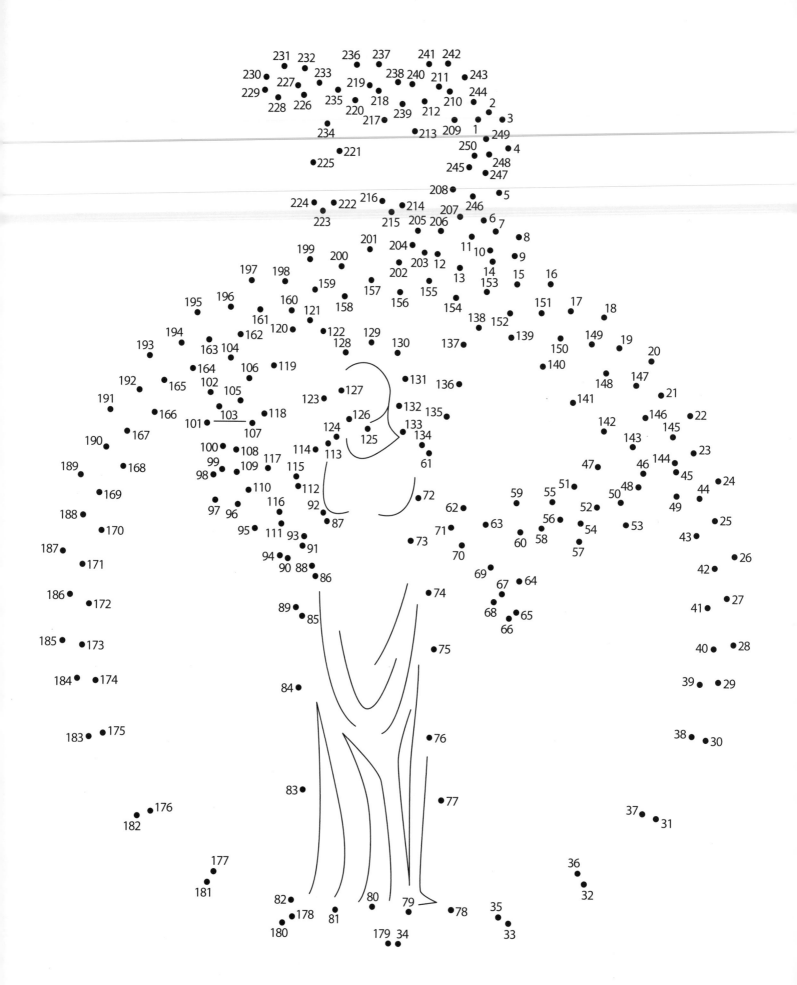

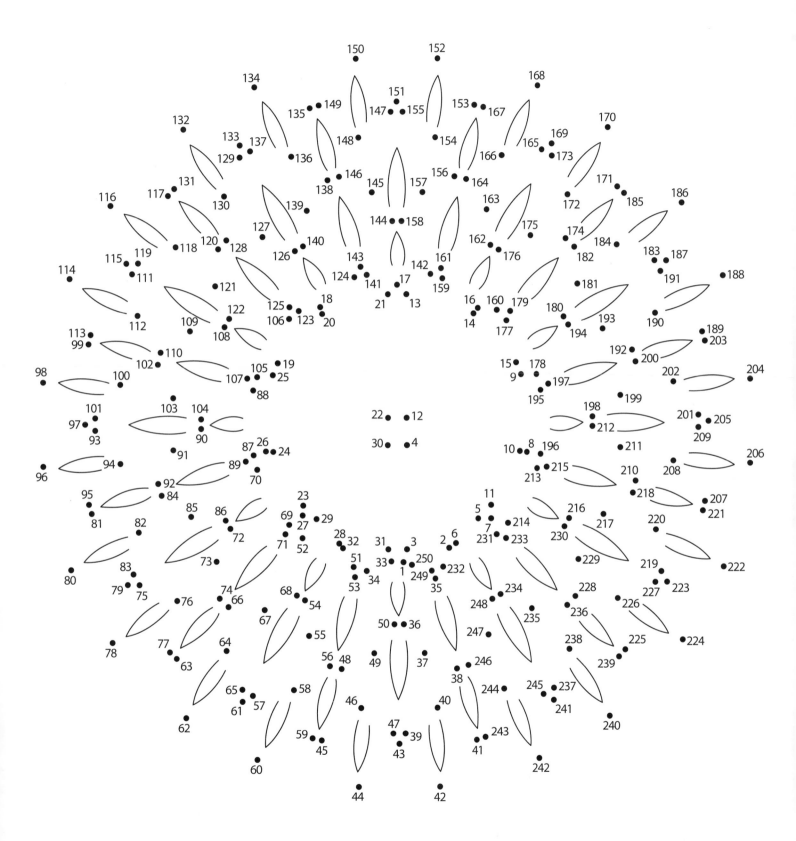

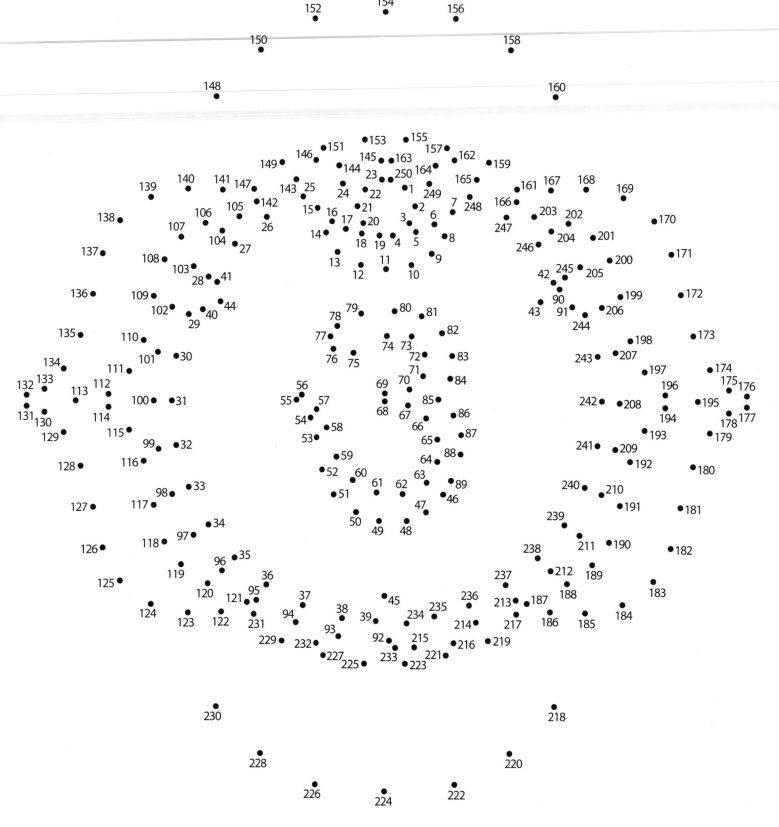

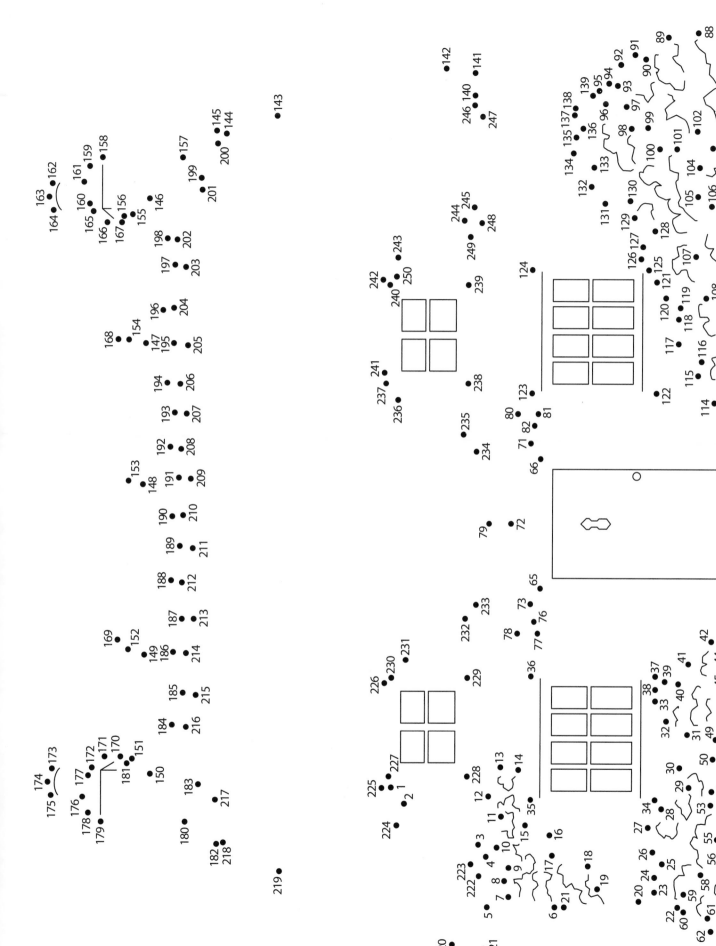

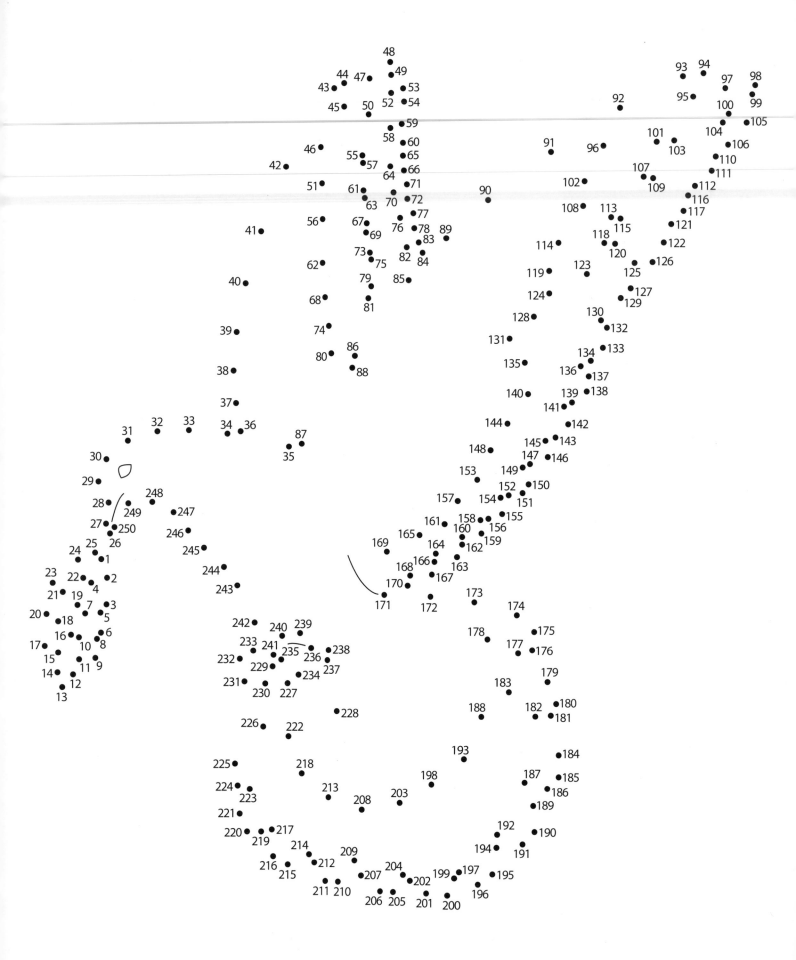

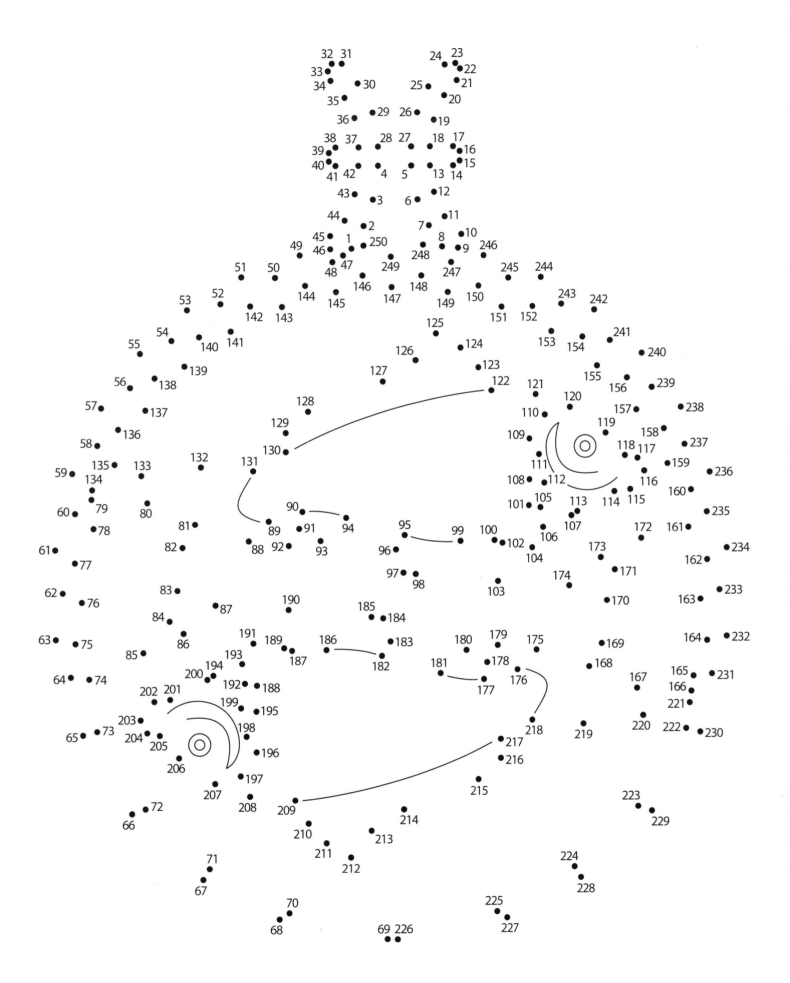

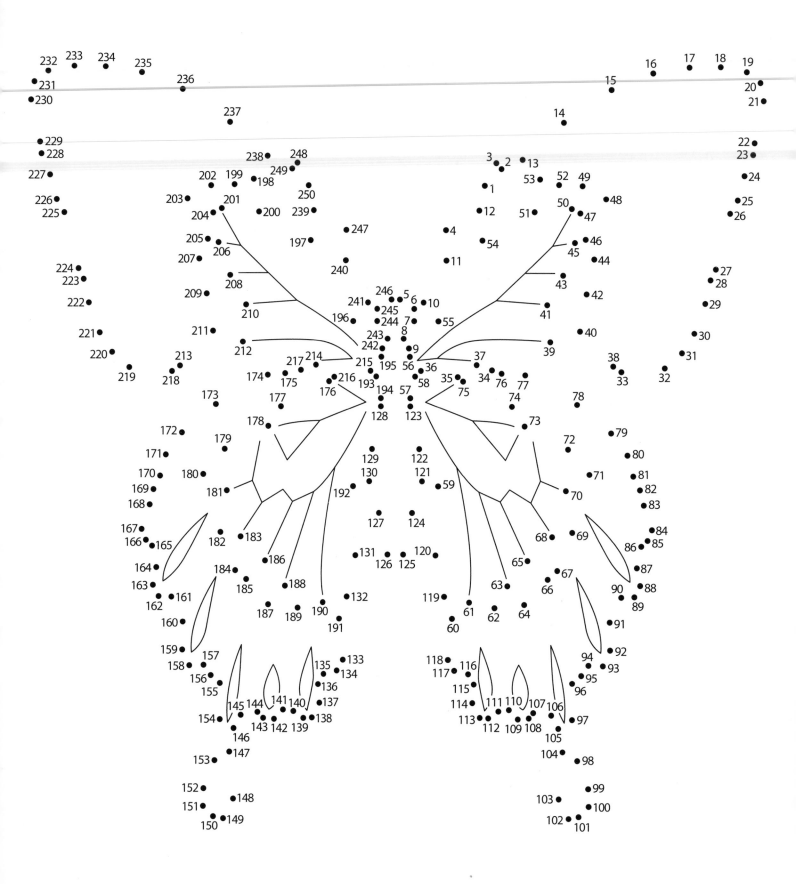

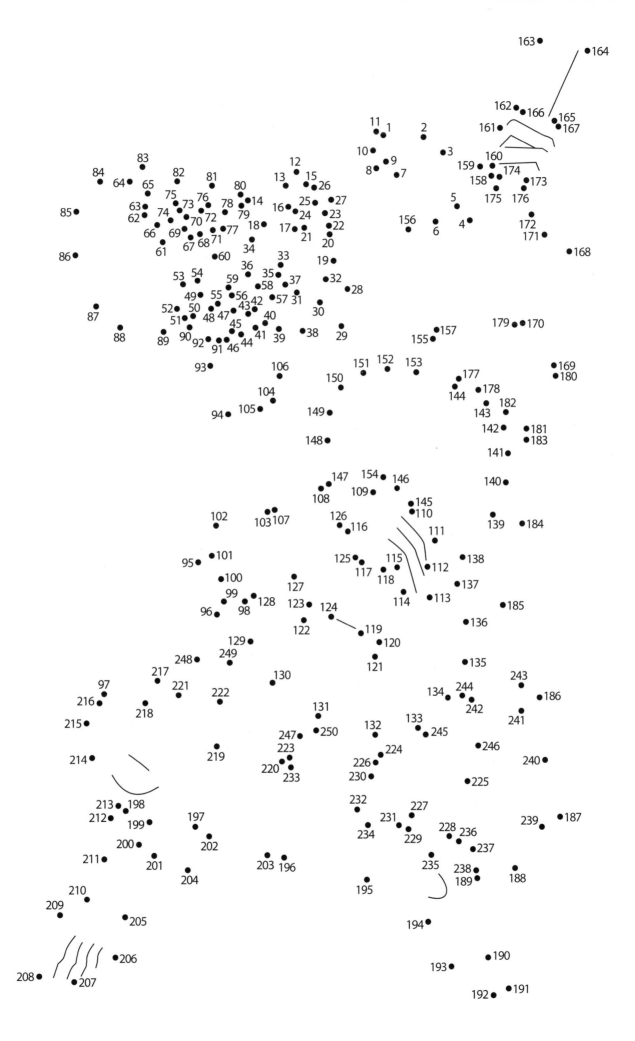

List of illustrations